'C' PROGRAMMING – A PRACTICAL PERSPECTIVE

Dr. Sachin Kadam
Director – MCA
Sinhgad Institute of Management and
Computer Application (SIMCA), Pune.

Prof. Gauri (Ranadive) Madan
Lecturer
MCA (Master of Computer Application)
MAEER'S Arts, Commerce & Science College,
Pune.

First Edition : 2011

Himalaya Publishing House

MUMBAI • NEW DELHI • NAGPUR • BENGALURU • HYDERABAD • CHENNAI • PUNE • LUCKNOW • AHMEDABAD • ERNAKULAM • BHUBANESWAR • INDORE • KOLKATA • GUWAHATI

First Edition : 2011

Published by : Mrs. Meena Pandey for **Himalaya Publishing House Pvt. Ltd.**, "Ramdoot", Dr. Bhalerao Marg, Girgaon, **Mumbai - 400 004.** Phone: 022-23860170/23863863, Fax: 022-23877178 **E-mail: himpub@vsnl.com; Website: www.himpub.com**

Branch Offices :

New Delhi : "Pooja Apartments", 4-B, Murari Lal Street, Ansari Road, Darya Ganj, New Delhi - 110 002. Phone: 011-23270392, 23278631; Fax: 011-23256286

Nagpur : Kundanlal Chandak Industrial Estate, Ghat Road, Nagpur - 440 018. Phone: 0712-2738731, 3296733; Telefax: 0712-2721215

Bengaluru : No. 16/1 (Old 12/1), 1st Floor, Next to Hotel Highlands, Madhava Nagar, Race Course Road, Bengaluru - 560 001. Phone: 080-32919385; Telefax: 080-22286611

Hyderabad : No. 3-4-184, Lingampally, Besides Raghavendra Swamy Matham, Kachiguda, Hyderabad - 500 027. Phone: 040-27560041, 27550139; Mobile: 09848130433

Chennai : No. 85/50, Bazullah Road, T. Nagar, Chennai - 600 017. Phone: 044-28144004/28144005

Pune : First Floor, "Laksha" Apartment, No. 527, Mehunpura, Shaniwarpeth (Near Prabhat Theatre), Pune - 411 030. Phone: 020-24496323/24496333

Lucknow : Jai Baba Bhavan, Church Road, Near Manas Complex and Dr. Awasthi Clinic, Aliganj, Lucknow - 226 024. Phone: 0522-2339329, 4068914; Mobile: 09305302158, 09415349385, 09389593752

Ahmedabad : 114, "SHAIL", 1st Floor, Opp. Madhu Sudan House, C.G. Road, Navrang Pura, Ahmedabad - 380 009. Phone: 079-26560126; Mobile: 09327324149, 09314679413

Ernakulam : 39/104 A, Lakshmi Apartment, Karikkamuri Cross Rd., Ernakulam, Cochin - 622011, Kerala. Phone: 0484-2378012, 2378016; Mobile: 09344199799

Bhubaneswar : 5 Station Square, Bhubaneswar (Odisha) - 751 001. Mobile: 09861046007

Indore : Kesardeep Avenue Extension, 73, Narayan Bagh, Flat No. 302, IIIrd Floor, Near Humpty Dumpty School, Narayan Bagh, Indore - 452 007 (M.P.). Mobile: 09301386468

Kolkata : 108/4, Beliaghata Main Road, Near ID Hospital, Opp. SBI Bank, Kolkata - 700 010, Phone: 033-32449649, Mobile: 09910440956

Guwahati : House No. 15, Behind Pragjyotish College, Near Sharma Printing Press, P.O. Bharalumukh, Guwahati - 781009. (Assam). Mobile: 09883055590, 09883055536

DTP by : Prerana Enterprises, Mumbai

Printed by : A to Z Printer, New Delhi.

PREFACE

We have had a love/hate relationship with C for years. We love the ease with which one can write C programs. We love the development environments that come with many of today's C compilers. But we hate the ease with which one can make mistakes. We hate the attention to picky details that C programming often requires. And above all, we hate the way many C programmers disparage other languages. Let's face it: C is not the ultimate programming language (no other language either). It is, however, a language with which every software developer should become familiar. It has become, for better or for worse, the *lingua franca* of the computer world. The present book is an attempt to bring this *lingua franca* closer to would be computer professionals.

This book is designed as a primary text for a C course. Previous programming experience in a high-level language is helpful, but not necessary for a computer-literate reader. Since the book is self-contained and usable for reference as well as learning, it makes an excellent companion text for a course in data structures, compiler design, operating systems, computer graphics, or other courses that use C as programming language. Due to its ample collection of programs, exercises and emphasis on practical problems, the book will also appeal to readers who are enrolled in a training class or who are learning C by self-study.

This book has been designed with the following goals in mind;

- Be clear, readable and entertaining
- Be accessible to a broad range of readers
- Be authoritative without being pedantic
- Be organized for easy teaching and learning
- Emphasize style
- Avoid dependence on a particular machine, compiler or operating system
- Use illustrations to clarify key concepts

While making sure to achieve the above mentioned goals, we have also incorporated certain features in the book which the readers will certainty appreciate;

- Illustrated programs: Choosing illustrative programs is not an easy job. If programs are too brief and artificial, readers will not get any sense of how the features are used in the real world. On the other hand, if a program is too realistic, its point can easily be lost in a forest of details. We have chosen a middle course, using small, simple examples to make concepts clear when they are first introduced, then gradually building up the complexity
- Exercises: Each chapter ends with a series of questions related to material covered in the chapter. Topics addressed in these sections include Frequently Asked Questions (FAQs).

The book is divided into four parts:

Part - I:

Chapter 1: Algorithms and Flowcharts

Chapter 2: Introduction to C

Chapter 3: Tokens and Data Types

Chapter 4: Operators and Expressions

Chapter 5: Control Statements

Part-II:

Chapter 6: Preprocessor

Chapter 7: Input and Output

Chapter 8: Functions

Chapter 9: Arrays

Part-III:

Chapter 10: Pointers

Chapter 11: Structures and Unions

Chapter 12: File Management

Part-IV:

Appendix-I: A complete list of ASCII symbols

Appendix-II: A complete list of C keywords and operators

Appendix-III: A header-file wise listing of all functions in the C library

We hope that the reader will enjoy the book the same way we enjoyed writing it.

Dr. Sachin Kadam

Prof. Gauri (Ranadive) Madan

Contents

PART – II

PART – III

PART – IV

PART – I

1. Algorithms and Flowcharts
2. Introduction to C Programming
3. Tokens and Data Types
4. Operators and Expressions
5. Control Statement

1

ALGORITHMS AND FLOWCHARTS

OBJECTIVE

In this chapter you will learn Algorithm, Flowchart, and Characteristics of Algorithm, Control structure in Algorithm, Flow chart Symbols

1.1 Problem Solving with Computers

The computer always demands unambiguous definition of the problem, which is simple to carry out and straight forward to implement in order to solve the problem. At this level the programmer is assumed to have certain amount of background knowledge, reasoning skills and hints for problem solving.

Steps involved in problem solving using computers are :

- Make a closer study of given problem and analyze it
- Redefine the problem if necessary
- Specify what is expected as an outcome of processing
- Find a suitable solution method to solve the given problem
- Based on above analysis, formulate a set of steps or procedural steps (known as Algorithm) of the chosen method of solution

- Express the algorithm in precise notation, feed it to computer, compute the results and reevaluate it
- Repeat the above steps till you get correct solution of given problem.

1.2 Algorithms

The finite set of procedural steps, where each step is precise, unambiguous and capable of being carried out by a machine in a finite time is known as **Algorithm**. As computer expects unambiguous, precise and definite instructions or command to solve a problem so the algorithm must be expressed in a 'precise notation'. An algorithm when it is expressed in one of the precise notation is called as a computer program. Before writing the computer program from algorithm an intermediate step, i.e., flowcharting is needed.

1.3 Flowchart

A flowchart is the pictorial representation of algorithmic steps to be performed sequentially to arrive at the result. Actually the computer program is written only after writing the flowchart.

Statement: Find sum and average of three numbers and print the result

Redefined problem: Write a program to find the sum and average of 3 float number. Accept 3 numbers from standard input device and display the result on monitor, Outcome of process is sum and average of three numbers taken from input device.

(1) Algorithm to add 3 numbers and prints sum and average.

Step 1. [First input the 3 numbers]
Input a, b, c

Step 2. [Finding the sum of given numbers]
Sum <— (a+b+c)

Step 3. [Finding the average]
Average <— sum/3.0

Step 4. [Print the results]
Write sum, average

Step 5. [End of the algorithm]
End

1.4 Characteristics of Algorithms

1.4.1. Input

Algorithm starts with a procedural step to accept input data. The subsequent steps in the algorithm process these data elements. But this input step is optional and is used only when the algorithm needs data at the time of execution.

1.4.2. Definite

Each operational step must be definite, i.e., it should specify what should be done. In other words there should not be any confusing instruction.

For example: (1) "Compute 5/0"

(2) "Add 5 or 10 to 5"

Above statements are not allowed in algorithms because in first statement result of 5/0 is infinity which is not defined in Computers and also in all branches of Mathematics. The second statement, which one of the two numbers 5 or 10 should be added to 5, is not clear.

1.4.3. Effective

Each operation must be effective to carry out. Effectiveness property of an algorithm says that each operational step can be at least in principle, being carried in a minimum amount of time.

For example, analyze the mathematical formula given below

$Y = PX^3 + QX^2 + RX + S$

The above statement can be written as C - statement as follows

Y= (P*X*X*X)+(Q*X*X)+(R*X)+S;

But to execute the above statement, the computer has to do six multiplications and three additions. We can modify the above formulas as below i.e.

===> $Y=X\,(PX^2+QX+R)+S$

===> Y=X (X(PX+Q)+R)+S

In C-statement, this can be written as Y= X* (X* ((P* X) +Q) +R) +S.

Now there are only 3 multiplications and 3 additions. Therefore the above statement is more efficient and takes less time for execution. The computing speed decreases as we go from operations additions, subtractions, multiplication, divisions, power( ) functions, logarithmic calculations, trigonometric functions and other mathematical functions. Therefore one should try to replace slow operations by faster operations as far as possible.

For examples:

Replace pow (x, 3) by x*x*x

Replace 3*y by y+y+y

Replace n/2.0 by n*0.5

Also try to avoid the repetitions of operations.

For example:

Repeated operations (slow)	more efficient (fast)
Sum = a + b + c + d	sum = a + b + c + d
avg = (a + b + c + d)/4.0	avg = sum/4.0

1.4.4. Terminate

After some minimum number of operations, algorithm must come to an end, i.e., the total time to carry out all the steps in algorithm must be limited (finite).

1.4.5. Output

An algorithm is written to solve the problem therefore it must produce one or more computed results. In order to incorporate the definiteness property of the algorithm, algorithms will be expressed using a precise notation called programming languages. Such computer programming languages are designed to assign clarity, definiteness and effectiveness to each of the instructions of the algorithm. The languages actually consist of all necessary features to support the characteristics of an algorithm.

1.5 Basic Control Structures in Algorithms

Usually the algorithm consists of finite set of sequential procedural steps. The algorithm may have conditions, which are used to take decision, and depending upon decisions, a particular group of statements are selected for execution. There are also situations in which some of the statements have to be executed repeatedly. So to meet above situations of problem solving, algorithm uses 3 basic forms of control structures;

1.5.1 Sequencing

1.5.2 Branching (selections)

1.5.3 Repetitions (looping)

These are also called as program structures used in developing structured programs.

1.5.1 Sequencing

The sequence structure indicates the sequential flow of program logic, i.e., step by step execution of program statements in the algorithm.

For example:

(1) In algorithm:

Step 1: [Input the three numbers]
Input n1, n2, n3

Step 2: [Multiply given numbers and store the result in another variable]
Mult ← n1*n2*n3

Step 3: [Add all numbers and store the sum in another variable]
Sum ← n1+n2+n3

(2) In Flowchart:

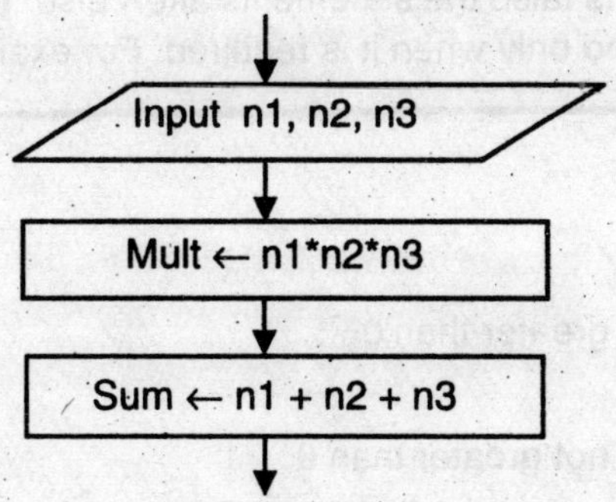

(3) In C program:

```
.
.
scanf("%d%d%d",&n1,&n2,&n3);
mult=n1*n2*n3;
sum=n1+n2+n3;
.
```

The step-by-step execution of statements in the algorithm (or in flowchart, programs) is known as sequencing or sequential execution.

1.5.2. Branching (Selections)

Execution of a group of statements depending upon the given condition is known as branching or selection. In algorithm if-then-else statement is used for branching (selection). Its syntax is as follows:

```
if (condition) then
    statement-1
    statement-2
    -
    -
else
    statement-a
    statement-b
```

Here the condition is evaluated first and if the condition is true, the statements after "then" are executed and if condition is false the statements after "else" part are executed. Here the "else" part is optional and this is used only when it is required. For example:

(1) In Algorithm:

(a) if (a>0) then

write "A is greater than 0"

else

write "A is not greater than 0"

← x+A

(b) if (a>0) then

write "A is +ve number"

← x + a

(2) In Flowchart:

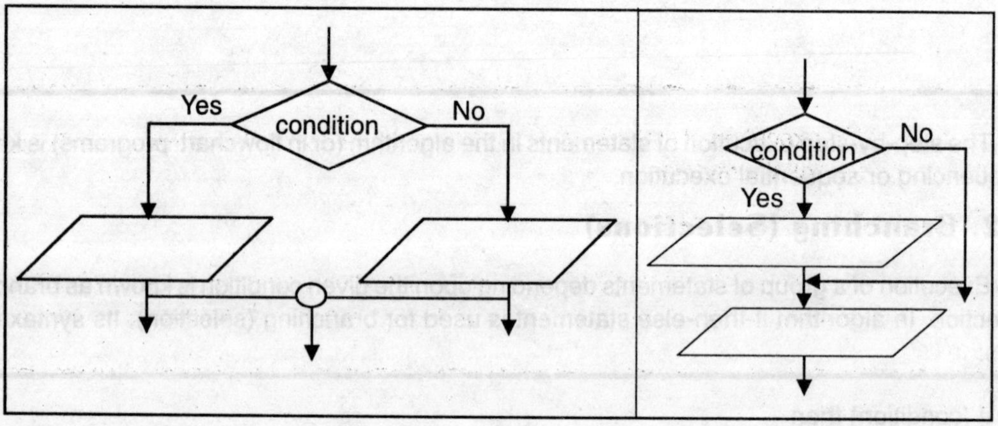

1.5.3. Repetitions (looping)

The repetitive execution of a group of statements or program segment takes place as long as the loop condition is true and when the loop condition becomes false, the loop or repetition will be terminated. This process is known as repetition or looping.

(1) In algorithms, repeat, for, do-while etc are used for looping.

Ex: Algorithm for finding sum and numbers from 1 to N

Step 1: [Input numbers]
Input N

Step 2: [Initialize the variable sum to zero]
Sum ← 0

Step 3: [Calculate the sum by looping]
Do
  Sum ← Sum+N
  N ← N-1
while N>0

Step 4: [Print the sum of numbers]
Write Sum

Step 5: [End of the algorithm]
End

(2) In Flowchart:

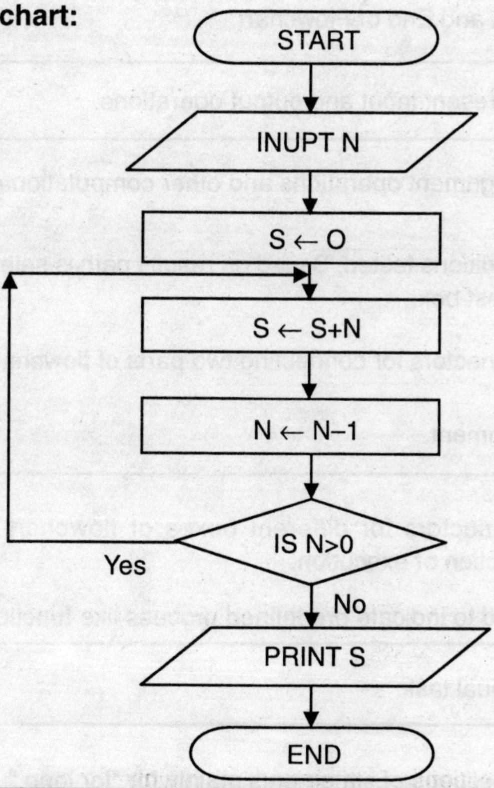

(3) In C programs:

```
main()
{
    int n,sum=0;
    do
    {
            sum+=n;
            n – –;
    } while(n>0);
    printf("\n The sum is %d",sum);
}
```

1.6 Flowchart Symbols

Symbol	Meaning
	Start and End of Flowchart.
	Represent input and output operations.
	Assignment operations and other computational operations.
	Conditions tested. Based on results path is selected. Also called as test box.
	Connectors for connecting two parts of flowcharts.
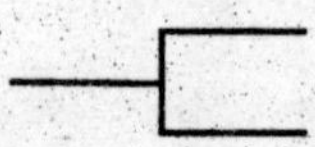	Comment.
	Connectors for different boxes of flowchart and shows the direction of execution.
	Used to indicate predefined process like functions in C.
	Manual task.
	Repetitions of statements mainly for "for loop."

1.7 Pseudocode

Flowcharts were the first design tool to be widely used, but unfortunately they do not very well reflect some of the concepts of structured programming. Pseudocode, on the other hand, is a newer tool and has features that make it more reflective for the structured concepts. Unfortunately, the narrative presentation is not as easy to understand and follow.

1.7.1 Rules for Pseudocode

(1) Write only one statement per line

(2) Each statement in your pseudocode should express just one action for the computer. If the task list is properly drawn, then in most cases each task will correspond to one line of pseudocode

(3) Capitalize keywords

(4) Indent to show hierarchy

We will use a particular indentation pattern in each of the design structures

SEQUENCE: keep statements that are "stacked" in sequence all starting in the same column

SELECTION: indent the statements that fall inside the selection structure, but not the keywords that form the selection

LOOPING: indent the statements that fall inside the loop, but not the keywords that form the loop

(5) End multiline structures

(6) Keep statements language independent

Resist the urge to write in whatever language you are most comfortable with. In the long run, you will save time! There may be special features available in the language you plan to eventually write the program in; if you are SURE it will be written in that language, then you can use the features. If not, then avoid using the special features.

Selection:

The pseudocode for this would be:

```
IF amount < 1000
interestRate = 0.06
ELSE
interestRate = 0.10
ENDIF
```

Looping:

The pseudocode for this would be:

```
count = 0
WHILE count < 10
```

```
ADD 1 to count
WRITE count
ENDWHILE
WRITE "The end"
```

1.7.2 Advantages and Disadvantages

Pseudocode Disadvantages

(1) It's not visual

(2) There is no accepted standard, so it varies widely from company to company

Pseudocode Advantages

(1) Can be done easily on a word processor

(2) Easily modified

(3) Implements structured concepts well

Flowchart Disadvantages

(1) Hard to modify

(2) Need special software (not so much now!)

(3) Structured design elements not all implemented

Flowchart Advantages

(1) Standardized: all pretty much agree on the symbols and their meaning

(2) Visual (but this does bring some limitations)

1.8 System Flowcharts

A system flowchart is a flowchart which gives overall view of computer system in addition to the pictorial representation of the flow of operations of an algorithm.

In other words as the name itself indicates, system flowcharts are drawn to show diagrammatically, the total environment of computer system on which the given algorithm or program is to be solved. System flowcharts provide us a list of special symbols for indicating input-output devices on which data transactions are read/printed. Thereby one will get a clear picture of input/output devices connected to a computer system. Therefore system flowchart will further improve and assist the computer programming; because system flowcharts not only specify the operations to be performed pictorially but the computer system environment at which all these data processing activities are handled.

To summarize, a system flowchart is a graphical representation that gives the complete view of a data processing system. It has flowchart symbols to show the following:

The activities (either manual or computing) are carried out within such a data processing system. The I/O devices and storage media used to store/handle the data file, transactions, etc., are involved in data processing activities.

1.9. Some examples on Algorithms and Flowcharts

(1) Write and algorithm to accept temperature in Fahrenheit scale and convert into Celsius scale and draw a flowchart.

Formula: C = (F-32)/1.8 where F is Fahrenheit value and C is Celsius value.

Algorithm : Temperature conversion from Fahrenheit value to Celsius value.

Step 1: [Input temperature in Fahrenheit scale]

Input F

Step 2: [Compute centigrade temperature]

C ← (F-32)/1.8

Step 3: [Print the result]

Write "Equivalent temperature in Celsius scale is", C

Step 5: [End of algorithm]

End

Flowchart:

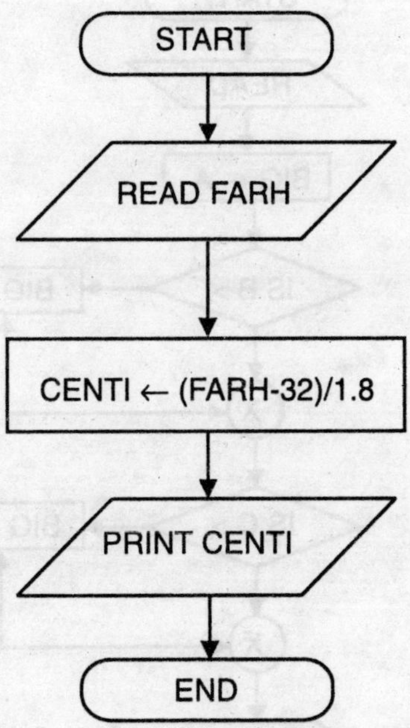

(2) Write an algorithm to find biggest of three numbers and draw the flowchart.

Algorithm: Finding the biggest of three numbers

Step 1: [Input three numbers from input device]
Input a,b,c

Step 2: [Store the first number in variable big assuming it as the biggest number]
Big ← a

Step 3: [Compare second value with big]
If b > big then big ← b

Step 4: [Compare second value with big]
If c > big then big ← c

Step 5: [Print the results]
Write "Biggest number is", big

Step 6: [End of the algorithm]
End

Flowchart:

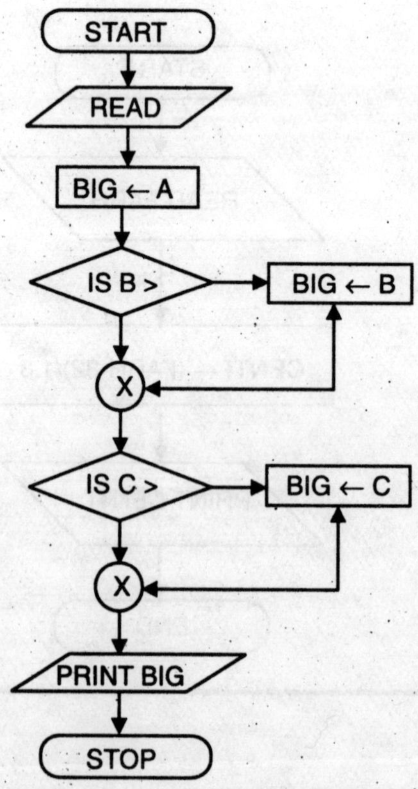

(3) Write an algorithm to find the factorial of a number and also draw the flowchart.

Algorithm : To find the factorial of a given number

Step 1: [Input the number]
Input N

Step 2: [Initialize the factorial number to 1]
Fact ← 1

Step 3: [Calculate factorial by looping]
Repeat for I=1 to N steps 1
Fact ← Fact * I
Loop

Step 4: [Print the factorial value]
Write "Factorial of",N, "is",fact

Step 5: [End of the algorithm]
End

Flowchart:

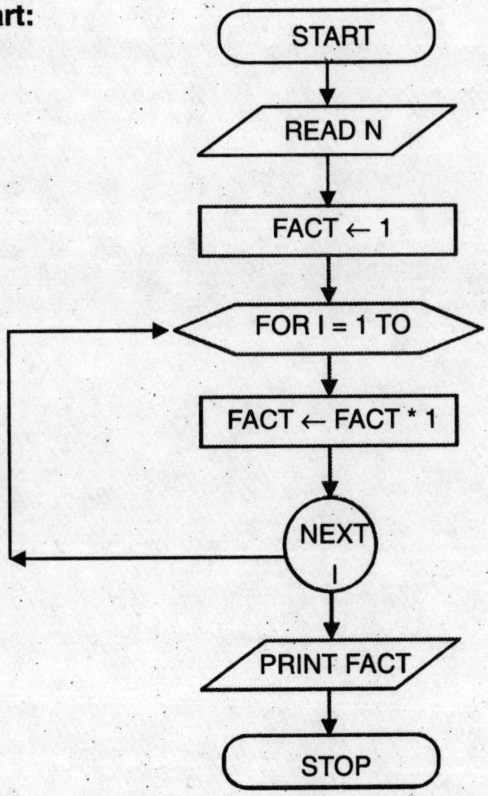

EXERCISE

(1) Explain these important terms :

(a) Algorithm

(b) Flowchart

(c) System Flowchart

(2) What is the difference between a flowchart and a system flowchart ?

(3) Why are flowcharts usually used to describe algorithms instead of written descriptions ?

(4) Flowcharts can also be used to describe activities that humans carry out. Draw a flowchart for one of these activities :

(a) Making a telephone call. *(b)* Making a cup of tea. *(c)* Repairing a bicycle tyre.

(5) Choose an information system such as a spreadsheet or database that you have created. Draw either a system flowchart or a flowchart to explain how the system operates.

■ ■ ■

2

INTRODUCTION TO C

OBJECTIVE

This chapter is designed to give you a general overview of the C programming language, Edit, link and run your C programs, C character set and the general structure of a C program

2.1 A Brief History of C

C is a general-purpose language which has been closely associated with the UNIX operating system for which it was developed - since the system and most of the programs that run it are written in C. Many of the important ideas of C stem from the language BCPL, developed by Martin Richards. The influence of BCPL on C proceeded indirectly through the language B, which was written by Ken Thompson in 1970 at Bell Labs, for the first UNIX system on a DEC PDP-7. BCPL and B are "type less" languages whereas C provides a variety of data types. In 1972 Dennis Ritchie at Bell Labs writes C and in 1978 the publication of The C Programming Language by Kernighan & Ritchie caused a revolution in the computing world. In 1983, the American National Standards Institute (ANSI) established a committee to provide a modern, comprehensive definition of C. The resulting definition, the ANSI standard, or "ANSI C", was completed late 1988.A Rough Guide to Programming Languages is available on-line for those of you that are interested.

2.2 C Is Usually First

The programming language C was originally developed by Dennis Ritchie of Bell Laboratories and was designed to run on a PDP-11 with a UNIX operating system. Although it was originally intended to run under UNIX, there has been a great interest in running it under the MS-DOS operating system on the IBM PC and compatibles. It is an excellent language for this environment because of the simplicity of expression, the compactness of the code, and the wide range of applicability. Also, due to the simplicity and ease of writing a C compiler, it is usually the first high level language available on any new computer, including microcomputers, minicomputers, and mainframes. C is not the best beginning language because it is somewhat cryptic in nature. It allows the programmer a wide range of operations from high level down to a very low level, approaching the level of assembly language. There seems to be no limit to the flexibility available. One experienced C programmer made the statement, "You can program anything in C", and the statement is well supported by my own experience with the language. Along with the resulting freedom however, you take on a great deal of responsibility because it is very easy to write a program that destroys itself due to the silly little errors that a good Pascal compiler will flag and call a fatal error. In C, you are very much on your own as you will soon find. In order to successfully complete C programming language, I will begin with the most basic concepts of C and take you up to the highest level of C programming including the concepts of pointers, structures, and dynamic allocation. Programming in C is a tremendous asset in those areas where you may want to use Assembly Language but would rather keep it a "simple to write" and "easy to maintain" program. Even though the C language enjoys a good record when programs are transported from one implementation to another, there are differences in compilers that you will find anytime you try to use another compiler. Most of the differences become apparent when you use nonstandard extensions such as calls to the DOS BIOS when using MS-DOS, but even these differences can be minimized by careful choice of programming constructs.

2.3 ANSI-C Standard

When it became evident that the C programming language was becoming a very popular language available on a wide range of computers, a group of concerned individuals met to propose a standard set of rules for the use of the C programming language. The group represented all sectors of the software industry and after many meetings, and many preliminary drafts, they finally wrote an acceptable standard for the C language. It has been accepted by the American National Standards Institute (ANSI), and by the International Standards Organization (ISO). It is not forced upon any group or user, but since it is so widely accepted, it would be economic suicide for any compiler writer to refuse to conform to the standard. C is often called a "Middle Level" programming language. This is not a reflection on its lack of programming power but more a reflection on its capability to access the system's low level functions. A middle level language, such as C, probably does not supply all the constructs found in high-languages - but it provides you with all the building blocks that you will need to produce the results you want!

2.4 Why use C?

C has been used successfully for every type of programming problem imaginable from operating systems to spreadsheets to expert systems - and efficient compilers are available for machines ranging in power from the Apple Macintosh to the supercomputers. The largest measure of C's success seems to be based on purely practical considerations like:

- the portability of the compiler
- the standard library concept
- a powerful and varied repertoire of operators
- an elegant syntax
- ready access to the hardware when needed

2.5 Uses of C

C was initially used for system development work, in particular the programs that make-up the operating system. Some examples of the use of C might be:

- Operating Systems
- Language Compilers
- Assemblers
- Text Editors
- Print Spoolers
- Network Drivers
- Utilities

In recent years C has been used as a general-purpose language because of its popularity with programmers. It is not the world's easiest language to learn and you will certainly benefit if you are not learning C as your first programming language

2.6 C for Personal Computers

With regards to personal computers Microsoft C for IBM PC's. And Borland's C is seen to be the two most commonly used systems. However, the latest version of Microsoft C is now considered to be the most powerful and efficient C compiler for personal computers.

Running C Programs

This section is primarily aimed at the beginner who has no or little experience of using compiled languages.

The Edit-Compile-Link-Execute Process

Developing a program in a compiled language such as C requires at least four steps:

writing the program

compiling it

linking it

executing it

We will now cover each step separately.

Editing

You write a computer program with words and symbols that are understandable to human being. This is the *editing* part of the development cycle. You type the program directly into a window on the screen and save the resulting text as a separate file. This is often referred to as the *source file*. The custom is that the text of a C program is stored in a file with the extension .c for C programming language

Compiling

You cannot directly execute the source file. To run on any computer system, the source file must be translated into binary numbers understandable to the computer's Central Processing Unit . This process produces an intermediate object file - with the extension .obj.

Linking

Many compiled languages come with library routines which can be added to your program. These routines are written by the manufacturer of the compiler to perform a variety of tasks, from input/output to complicated mathematical functions. In the case of C the standard input and output functions are contained in a library (stdio.h). So even the most basic program will require a library function. After linking the file extension is .exe.

Executable files

Thus the text editor produces .c source files, which go to the compiler, producing .obj object files, which go to the linker, producing .exe executable file. You can then run .exe files as you can other applications, simply by typing their names at the DOS prompt or run using windows menu.

Using Microsoft C

Edit stage:

Type program in using one of the Microsoft Windows editing packages.

Compile and link:

Select Building from Make menu. Building option allows you to both compile and link in the same option.

Execute:

Use the Run menu and select Go option.

Errors:

First error highlighted. Use Next Error from Search menu for further errors if applicable. If you get an error message, or you find that the program does not work when you finally run it you will have to go back to the source file - the .c file - to make changes and go through the whole development process again!

Unix systems

man cc

on your local Unix system for more information.

Please note that Unix is a case sensitive operating system and files named firstprog.c and FIRSTPROG.c are treated as two separate files on these system. By default the Unix system compiles and links a program in one step, as follows:

cc firstprog.c

This command creates an executable file called a.out that overwrites any existing file called a.out. Executable files on Unix are run by typing their name. In this case the program is run as follows:

a.out

To change the name of the executable file type:

cc -o firstprog firstprog.c

This produces an executable file called firstprog

2.7 C Character Set

C does not use, nor requires the use of, every character found on a modern computer keyboard. The only characters required by the C Programming Language are as follows:

```
A - Z
a -z
0 - 9
space . , : ; ' $ '
# % & ! _ {} [] () < > |
+ - / * =
```

2.8 The form of a C Program

All C programs will consist of at least one function, but it is usual to write a C program that comprises several functions. The only function that has to be present is the function called main. The main function is the first function that is called when your program executes.

The layout of C Program

The general form of a C program is as follows

```
Pre-processor directives
global declarations
main()
{
  local variables to function main ;
  statements associated with function main ;
}
Userfunction1()
{
  local variables to function 1 ;
  statements associated with function 1 ;
}
......
......
etc
```

A very common mistake made by everyone, who is new to the C programming language, is to miss the semicolon.

2.9 Pre-processor Directives

C is a small language but provides the programmer with all the tools to be able to write powerful programs. C uses library of standard functions which are included when we build our programs. All pre-processor directives begin with a # and they must start in the first column. The commonest directive to all C programs is:

```
#include <stdio.h>
```

Note the use of the angle brackets (< and >) around the header's name. These indicate that the header file is to be looked for on the system disk which stores the rest of the C program application.

```
#include "stdio.h"
```

The double quotes indicate that the current working directory should be searched for the required header file.

The program is a short one, to say the least. Here it is:

```
#include <stdio.h>
main()
{
   printf("Hello World\n");
}
```

The first line is the standard start for all C programs - main(). After this comes the program's only instruction enclosed in curly brackets {}. The curly brackets mark the start and end of the list of instructions that make up the program.

Add Comments to a Program

A comment is a note to yourself or others that you put into your source code. All comments are ignored by the compiler. Comments are used primarily to document the meaning and purpose of your source code, so that you can remember later how it functions and how to use it.

In C, the start of a multiline comment is signalled by the /* character pair. A comment is ended by */. For example, this is a syntactically correct C comment:

/* This is a comment.

Used for multiline*/

In C, the start of a single line comment is signalled by the //

// This is single line comment

EXERCISE

(1) How do you execute a C program in MS-DOS?

(2) What is the statement terminator in C?

(3) Is the C language case sensitive or not?

(4) What do you mean by predefined?

(5) Explain the structure of a C program?

Program 2.1

```
/* The Hello program.c — The most famous program of them all... */
#include <stdio.h>
int main(void)
  {
  printf("Hello World!\n");
  }
```

■ ■ ■

3 TOKENS AND DATA TYPES

OBJECTIVE

In this chapter you will learn C Tokens, Keywords, Variable, Constant, and Data types, Size of each type and where to use these Data Types. Storage Class: Visibility of the Variable

3.1 C Tokens

In a passage of text, individual words and punctuation marks are called tokens. Similarly, in C program, the smallest individual units are known as C tokens. C has following tokens:

(1) Keywords or Reserve words such as float, int, etc.

(2) Constants such as 1,15,5 etc.

(3) Identifiers such as name, amount etc.

(4) Operators such as +, -, * etc.

(5) Separators such as :, ;, [,] etc. and special characters

(6) Strings

3.2 Keywords

Keywords or Reserve words of the C language are the words whose meaning is already defined and explained to the C language compiler. Therefore Reserve words cannot be used as identifiers or variable names. They should only be used to carry the pre-defined meaning. For example int is a reserve word. It indicates the data type of the variable as integer. Therefore it is reserved to carry the specific meaning. Any attempt to use it other than the intended purpose will generate a compile time error. C language has 32 keywords. Following are some of them:

Auto	break	Case	char	const	continue	default
Do	double	Else	enum	extern	float	for
Goto	if	Int	long	register	return	short
Signed	sizeof	Static	struct	switch	typedef	union
unsigned	void	Volatile	while			

3.3 Variables

A variable is a name given to the space in the memory for holding data such as integers, characters, floating point numbers, strings, etc. Using a variable name is more convenient than using the memory locations. There are certain rules for naming variables for which you need to refer to the rules for identifiers.

3.3.1 Declaration of variables

To declare a variable means to create a memory space for the variable depending on the data type used and associate the memory location with the variable name. In C all the variables should be declared before it can be used. Also you *cannot re-declare* a variable once it has been already declared.

The general pattern for declaring a variable is as follows:

e.g.:

```
int age;
int age, count, i, j;
float amount, rateofinterest, totalbalance;
char ch;
```

3.4 Constant Variables

Constant

A constant can be defined as "*a quantity that does not change during the execution of a program*".

```
#include <stdio.h>
int main(void)
{
        int a = 10;
        printf("%d",a);
}
Program Output
10
```

Here we are declaring a variable with its initial value 10. 10 here is an integer constant and every time you try to execute this program.

3.4.1 Types of Constants

3.4.1.1 Integer Constant

An integer constant must have at least one digit and should not have decimal point. It could either be positive or negative.

3.4.1.2 Real Constant

A real constant must have at least one digit and must have a decimal point.

3.4.1.3 Character Constant

A character constant should be only one character and must be enclosed in single quotes, e.g., 'A', 'b', etc. A constant variable is also called a named constant. A named constant is really a variable whose content is read-only and cannot be changed while the program is running. Here is a declaration of a named constant.

```
const float pi = 3.14;
```

"Symbolic constants" can be specified using the "define" C preprocessor declaration:

```
#define PI 3.141592654
```

There is also a "const" declaration that defines a read-only variable, such as a memory location in ROM:

```
const int a;
```

3.4.2 Defining Symbolic Constants

A symbolic constant value can be defined as a preprocessor statement and is used in the program as any other constant value. The general form of a symbolic constant is

```
# define symbolic_name value of constant
```

Valid examples of constant definitions are :

```
# define marks 100
# define total 50
# define pi 3.14159
```

These values may appear anywhere in the program, but must come before it is referenced in the program.

3.4.3 Declaring Variable as Constant

The values of some variable may be required to remain constant through-out the program. We can do this by using the qualifier const at the time of initialization.

Example: const int class_size = 40;

The const data type qualifier tells the compiler that the value of the int variable class_size may not be modified in the program.

3.4.4 Naming Constants and Variables

There are several rules that you must follow when naming constants and variables:

Names...	Example
Should not start with a number	2i
Should not be a C keyword	struct
Should not contain any arithmetic operators...	r*s+t
Should not contain any other punctuation marks...	#@x%£!!a
Should not contain a space	im stupid
CAN be of mixed cases	XSquared
CAN contain a number elsewhere	h2o
CAN contain or begin with an underscore	_height_

3.5 Storage Class

Variables in C have not only the data type but also storage class that provides information about their location and visibility. The storage class divides the portion of the program within which the variables are recognized.

3.5.1 auto : It is a local variable known only to the function in which it is declared. Auto is the default storage class.

3.5.2 static : Local variable which exists and retains its value even after the control is transferred to the calling function.

3.4.3 extern : Global variable known to all functions in the file

3.4.4 register : Social variables which are stored in the register.

[Storage classes are discussed more in detail in chapter function]

3.6 Data Types

C language data types can be broadly classified as

Primary data type

Derived data type

User-defined data type

3.6.1 Primary data type

All C Compilers accept the following fundamental data types

(1)	Integer	Int
(2)	Character	char
(3)	Floating Point	float
(4)	Double precision floating point	double
(5)	Void	void

The size and range of each data type is given in the table below

DATA TYPE	RANGE OF VALUES
char	-128 to 127
Int	-32768 to +32767
float	3.4 e-38 to 3.4 e+38
double	1.7 e-308 to 1.7 e+308

3.6.1.1 Integer Type :

Integers are whole numbers with a machine dependent range of values. A good programming language as to support the programmer by giving a control on a range of numbers and storage space. C has 3 classes of integer storage namely short int, int and long int. All of these data types have signed and unsigned forms. A short int requires half the space than normal integer values. Unsigned numbers are always positive and consume all the bits for the magnitude of the number. The long and unsigned integers are used to declare a longer range of values.

3.6.1.2 Floating Point Types :

Floating point number represents a real number with 6 digits precision. Floating point numbers are denoted by the keyword float. When the accuracy of the floating point number is insufficient, we can use the double to define the number. The double is same as float but with longer precision. To extend the precision further we can use long double which consumes 80 bits of memory space.

3.6.1.3 Void Type :

Using void data type, we can specify the type of a function. It is a good practice to avoid functions that does not return any values to the calling function.

3.6.1.4 Character Type :

A single character can be defined as a character type of data. Characters are usually stored in 8 bits of internal storage. The qualifier signed or unsigned can be explicitly applied to char. While unsigned characters have values between 0 and 255, signed characters have values from –128 to 127.

Size and Range of Data Types on 16 bit machine.

TYPE	SIZE (Bits)	Range
Char or Signed Char	8	-128 to 127
Unsigned Char	8	0 to 255
Int or Signed int	16	-32768 to 32767
Unsigned int	16	0 to 65535
Short int or Signed short int	8	-128 to 127
Unsigned short int	8	0 to 255
Long int or signed long int	32	-2147483648 to 2147483647
Unsigned long int	32	0 to 4294967295
Float	32	3.4 e-38 to 3.4 e+38
Double	64	1.7e-308 to 1.7e+308
Long Double	80	3.4 e-4932 to 3.4 e+4932

3.7 Declaration of Variables

Every variable used in the program should be declared to the compiler. The declaration does two things.

(1) Tells the compiler the variable name.

(2) Specifies what type of data the variable will hold.

The general format of any declaration

datatype var1, var2, var3, ……….. varn;

Where var1, var2, var3 are variable names. Variables are separated by commas. A declaration statement must end with a semicolon.

Example:

```
int sum;
int number, salary;
double average, mean;
```

Datatype	Keyword Equivalent
Character	char
Unsigned Character	unsigned char
Signed Character	signed char
Signed Integer	signed int (or) int
Signed Short Integer	signed short int (or) short int (or) short
Signed Long Integer	signed long int (or) long int (or) long
UnSigned Integer	unsigned int (or) unsigned
UnS'gned Short Integer	unsigned short int (or) unsigned short
UnSigned Long Integer	unsigned long int (or) unsigned long
Floating Point	float
Double Precision Floating Point	double
Extended Double Precision Floating Point	long double

3.8 User Defined Type Declaration

In C language a user can define an identifier that represents an existing data type. The user defined datatype identifier can later be used to declare variables.

The general syntax is

typedef type identifier;

here type represents existing data type and 'identifier' refers to the 'row' name given to the data type.

Example:

typedef int salary;

3.9 Special Data Type Enum

Defines a set of constants of type int.

The syntax for defining constants using enum is

enum [*tag*] {*name* [=*value*], ...};

The set can optionally be given a type tag name with *tag*. *name* is the name of a constant that can optionally be assigned the (constant) value, etc.

For example,

enum Numbers {One = 1, Two = 2, Three = 3, Four = 4, Five = 5};

If *value* is missing, then a value is assumed to be the value of the previous constant in the list + 1. If this is the first constant in the list, the default value is 0.

If you give a type tag name, then you can declare variables of enumerated type using

enum *tag variable-names*;

For example,

enum Numbers x, y, z;

declares three variables x, y and z, all of type *Numbers* (they are, infact, integer variables). More precise, 'enum *tag*' becomes a new type which is equal in rights with any built-in type.

3.10 Precedence

short <= int <= long

float <= double <= long double

There are a number of special characters called escape sequence defined in C. They are:

'\a'	alarm (beep) character
'\p'	backspace
'\f'	formfeed
'\n'	newline
'\r'	carriage return
'\t'	horizontal tab
'\v'	vertical tab
'\\'	backslash
'\?'	question mark
'\''	single quote
'\"'	double quote
'\0NN'	character code in octal
'\xNN'	character code in hex
'\0'	null character

Exercise

(1) What is static identifier?

(2) What are the types of tokens in C?

(3) What do you mean keyword?

(4) How many keywords are there in C?

(5) What is single character constant?

(6) What is string constant?

(7) What are escape sequences?

(8) What do you mean by initialization of variable?

(9) What does a static variable mean?

(10) What does the keyword "void" indicate?

Program 3.1

What are the values of TRUE and FALSE in C ?

```
#include <stdio.h>
int main(void)
 {
 printf("The value of 1<2 is %d\n", (1<2));
 printf("The value of 2<1 is %d\n", (2<1));
 }
```

The program prints out

The value of 1<2 is 1

The value of 2<1 is 0

Program 3.2

Various C features - __DATE__, sizeof, conditional expressions, ...c — various C constructs

```
#include <stdio.h>
int main(void)
 {
 int answer;
 short x = 1;
 long y = 2;
 float u = 3.0;
 double v = 4.4;
 long double w = 5.54;
 char c = 'p';;
/* __DATE__, __TIME__, __FILE__, __LINE__ are predefined symbols */
 printf("Date : %s\n", __DATE__);
 printf("Time : %s\n", __TIME__);
 printf("File : %s\n", __FILE__);
 printf("Line : %d\n", __LINE__);
 printf("Enter 1 or 0 : ");
 scanf("%d", &answer);
/* answer?"you said yes":"You said no" is a conditional expression */
```

```
  printf ("%s\n", answer? "You said YES": "You said NO");
/* The size of various types */
  printf("The size of int %d\n", sizeof(answer));
  printf("The size of short %d\n", sizeof(x));
  printf("The size of long %d\n", sizeof(y));
  printf("The size of float %d\n", sizeof(u));
  printf("The size of double %d\n", sizeof(v));
  printf("The size of long double %d\n", sizeof(w));
  printf("The size of char %d\n", sizeof(c));
  }
```

The output from a run was:

```
Date : Jun 27 2008
Time : 13:51:31
File : white.c
Line : 20
Enter 1 or 0 : 1
You said YES
The size of int 4
The size of short 2
The size of long 8
The size of float 4
The size of double 8
The size of long double 8
The size of char 1
```

■■■

4 Operators and Expressions

Objective

In this chapter you will learn Operators: Arithmetic Operators, Relational Operators, Logical Operators, Assignment Operators, Increments and Decrement Operators, Conditional Operators, Bitwise Operators and Special Operators.
Expression:

Arithmetic Expressions, Evaluation of Expressions, Precedence in Arithmetic Operators, Rules for evaluation of expression, Type conversions in expressions, Implicit type conversion, Explicit Conversion and Operator precedence and associativity.

4.1 Operators Introduction

An operator is a symbol which helps the user to command the computer to do certain mathematical or logical manipulations. Operators are used in C language program to operate on data and variables. C has a rich set of operators which can be classified as:

4.1.1. Arithmetic Operators

All the basic arithmetic operations can be carried out in C. Both unary and binary operations are available in C language. Unary operations operate on a singe operand and Binary operations operate on two operand

The following table shows the Arithmetic operators

here X, Y, Z are known as operands.

Operator	Meaning	Integer Arithmetic X=5, Y=3	Floating point Arithmetic X=5.0, Y=3.0
+	Addition or Unary Plus	X+Y =8	X+Y =8.0
–	Subtraction or Unary Minus	X-Y =2 OR –X-Y=-8	X-Y=2.0 OR –X-Y=-8.0
*	Multiplication	X*Y=15	X*Y=15.0
/	Division	X/Y=1	X/Y=1.66
%	Modulus Operator (Remainder)	X%Y=2	Not Applicable

4.1.1.1 Mixed mode arithmetic

When one of the operand is real and other is an integer and if the arithmetic operation is carried out on these 2 operands then it is called as mixed mode arithmetic. If any one operand is of real type then the result will always be real thus 15/10.0 = 1.5

4.1.2. Relational Operators

Often it is required to compare the relationship between operands and bring out a decision and program accordingly. This is when the relational operator come into picture and the evaluated value is always either TRUE or FALSE. C supports the following relational operators.

The following table shows the Arithmetic operators :

Operator	Meaning	Example exp1=5 and exp2=3 exp1 relational operator exp2
<	is less than	exp1 < exp2 .... FALSE
<=	is less than or equal to	exp1 <= exp2 ....FALSE
>	is greater than	exp1 > exp2 ....TRUE
>=	is greater than or equal to	exp1 >= exp2 ....TRUE
==	is equal to	exp1 == exp2 ....FALSE
!=	is not equal to	exp1 != exp2 ....TRUE

4.1.3. Logical Operators

C has the following logical operators, they compare or evaluate logical and relational expressions:

Operator	Meaning
&&	Logical AND
||	Logical OR
!	Logical NOT

Logical AND (&&)

This operator is used to evaluate 2 conditions or expressions with relational operators simultaneously. If both the expressions to the left and to the right of the logical operator is true then the whole compound expression is true.

Example :

a > b && x = = 10

The expression to the left is a > b and that on the right is x == 10 the whole expression is true only if both expressions are true i.e., if a is greater than b and x is equal to 10.

Logical OR (||)

The logical OR is used to combine 2 expressions or the condition evaluates to true if any one of the 2 expressions is true.

Example :

a < m || a < n

The expression evaluates to true if any one of them is true or if both of them are true. It evaluates to true if a is less than either m or n and when a is less than both m and n.

Logical NOT (!)

The logical not operator takes single expression and evaluates to true if the expression is false and evaluates to false if the expression is true. In other words it just reverses the value of the expression.

Example :

! (x >= y) the NOT expression evaluates to true only if the value of x is neither greater than or equal to y.

4.1.4. Assignment Operators

The Assignment Operator evaluates an expression on the right of the expression and substitutes it to the value or variable on the left of the expression. The commonly used shorthand assignment operators are as follows :

Assignment Operator	Statement with simple assignment operator	Statement with shorthand operator
+=	a = a + 1	a += 1
-=	a = a - 1	a -= 1
*=	a = a * (n+1)	a *= (n+1)
/=	a = a / (n+1)	a /= (n+1)
%=	a = a % b	a %= b

4.1.5. Increment and Decrement Operators

The increment and decrement operators are one of the unary operators which are very useful in C language. They are extensively used in for and while loops. The syntax of the operators are given below :

Increment and Decrement Operators	Prefix Notation	Postfix Notation
++	++X	X++
- -	- -Y	Y - -

The increment operator ++ adds the value 1 to the current value of operand and the decrement operator – – subtracts the value 1 from the current value of operand. The ++X and X++ mean the same thing when they form statements independently; they behave differently when they are used in expression on the right hand side of an assignment statement.

4.1.6. Conditional or Ternary Operator

The conditional operator consists of 2 symbols the question mark (?) and the colon (:) The syntax for a ternary operator is as follows

exp1 ? exp2 : exp3

The ternary operator works as follows

exp1 is evaluated first. If the expression is true then exp2 is evaluated & its value becomes the value of the expression. If exp1 is false, exp3 is evaluated and its value becomes the value of the expression. Note that only one of the expression is evaluated.

For example :

a = 10;

b = 15;

x = (a > b) ? a : b

Here x will be assigned to the value of b. The condition follows that the expression is false therefore b is assigned to x.

4.1.7. Bitwise Operators

C has a distinction of supporting special operators known as bitwise operators for manipulation data at bit level. A bitwise operator operates on each bit of data. Those operators are used for testing, complementing or shifting bits to the right or left. Bitwise operators may not be applied to a float or double.

Operator	Meaning
&	Bitwise AND
|	Bitwise OR
^	Bitwise Exclusive
<<	Shift left
>>	Shift right

4.1.8. Special Operators

C supports some special operators of interest such as comma operator, size of operator, pointer operators (& and *) and member selection operators (. and ->).

4.1.9. The Comma Operator

The comma operator can be used to link related expressions together. A comma-linked list of expressions are evaluated left to right and value of right most expression is the value of the combined expression.

For example the statement

value = (x = 10, y = 5, x + y);

First assigns 10 to x and 5 to y and finally assigns 15 to value. Since comma has the lowest precedence in operators the parenthesis is necessary. Some examples of comma operator are

In for loops:

for (n=1, m=10, n <=m; n++,m++)

In while loops

While (c=getchar(), c != '10')

Exchanging values

t = x, x = y, y = t;

4.1.10 The size of Operator

The operator size gives the size of the data type or variable in terms of bytes occupied in the memory. The operand may be a variable, a constant or a data type qualifier.

Example :

m = sizeof (sum);

The size of operator is normally used to determine the lengths of arrays and structures when their sizes are not known to the programmer. It is also used to allocate memory space dynamically to variables during the execution of the program.

4.2 Expressions

4.2.1 Arithmetic Expressions

An expression is a combination of variables constants and operators written according to the syntax of C language. In C every expression evaluates to a value, i.e., every expression results in some value of a certain type that can be assigned to a variable. Some examples of C expressions are shown in the table given below:

Algebraic Expression	C Expression
a x b – c	a * b – c
(m + n) (x + y)	(m + n) * (x + y)
(ab / c)	a * b / c
$3x^2$ +2x + 1	3*x*x+2*x+1
(x / y) + c	x / y + c

4.2.2. Evaluation of Expressions

Expressions are evaluated using an assignment statement form

Variable = expression;

Variable is any valid C variable name. When the statement is encountered, the expression is evaluated first and then replaces the previous value of the variable on the left hand side. All variables used in the expression must be assigned values before evaluation is attempted.

Example of evaluation statements are

x = a * b – c

y = b / c * a

z = a – b / c + d;

4.2.3 Precedence in Arithmetic Operators

An arithmetic expression without parenthesis will be evaluated from left to right using the rules of precedence of operators. There are two distinct priority levels of arithmetic operators in C.

High priority * / %

Low priority + -

4.2.4 Rules for evaluation of expression

First parenthesized sub expression left to right are evaluated.

If parentheses are nested, the evaluation begins with the innermost sub expression.

The precedence rule is applied in determining the order of application of operators in evaluating sub expressions. The associability rule is applied when two or more operators of the same precedence level appear in the sub expression. Arithmetic expressions are evaluated from left to right using the rules of precedence. When Parenthesis are used, the expressions within parenthesis assume highest priority.

4.3 Implicit Type Conversion

C permits mixing of constants and variables of different types in an expression. C automatically converts any intermediate values to the proper type so that the expression can be evaluated without loosing any significance. This automatic type conversion is known as implicit type conversion

The following rules apply during evaluating expressions

All short and char are automatically converted to int. Then

(1) If one operand is long double, the other will be converted to long double and result will be long double.

(2) If one operand is double, the other will be converted to double and result will be double.

(3) If one operand is float, the other will be converted to float and result will be float.

(4) If one of the operand is unsigned long int, the other will be converted into unsigned long int and result will be unsigned long int.

(5) If one operand is long int and other is unsigned int then

 (a) If unsigned int can be converted to long int, then unsigned int operand will be converted as such and the result will be long int.

 (b) Else both operands will be converted to unsigned long int and the result will be unsigned long int.

(6) If one of the operand is long int, the other will be converted to long int and the result will be long int.

(7) If one operand is unsigned int the other will be converted to unsigned int and the result will be unsigned int.

4.4 Explicit Conversion

Many times there may arise a situation where we want to force a type conversion in a way that is different from automatic conversion.

Consider for example the calculation of number of female and male students in a class

$$\text{Ratio} = \frac{\text{female students}}{\text{male students}}$$

Since if female students and male students are declared as integers, the decimal part will be rounded off and its ratio will represent a wrong figure. This problem can be solved by converting locally one of the variables to the floating point as shown below.

Ratio = (float) female students/male students

The operator float converts the female students to floating point for the purpose of evaluation of the expression. Then using the rule of automatic conversion, the division is performed by floating point mode, thus retaining the fractional part of the result. The process of such a local conversion is known as explicit conversion or casting a value. The general form is

(type_name) expression

4.5 Operator Precedence and Associativity

Each operator in C has a precedence associated with it. The precedence is used to determine how an expression involving more than one operator is evaluated. There are distinct levels of precedence and an operator may belong to one of these levels. The operators of higher precedence are evaluated first. The operators of same precedence are evaluated from right to left or from left to right depending on the level. This is known as associativity property of an operator.

The table given below gives the precedence of each operator.

Order	Category	Operator	Operation	Associativity
1	Highest precedence	( ) [ ] → : : .	Function call	L → R Left to Right
2	Unary	! ~ + - ++	Logical negation (NOT) Bitwise 1's complement Unary plus Unary minus Pre or post increment	R → L Right -> Left

<table>
<tr><th></th><th></th><th></th><th></th><th></th></tr>
<tr><td></td><td></td><td>- -
&
*
Size of</td><td>Pre or post decrement
Address
Indirection
Size of operant in bytes</td><td></td></tr>
<tr><td>3</td><td>Member Access</td><td>.*
→*</td><td>Dereference
Dereference</td><td>L → R</td></tr>
<tr><td>4</td><td>Multiplication</td><td>*
/
%</td><td>Multiply
Divide
Modulus</td><td>L → R</td></tr>
<tr><td>5</td><td>Additive</td><td>+
-</td><td>Binary______Plus
Binary Minus</td><td>L → R</td></tr>
<tr><td>6</td><td>Shift</td><td><<
>></td><td>Shifty______Left
Shift Right</td><td>L → R</td></tr>
<tr><td>7</td><td>Relational</td><td><
<=
>
>=</td><td>Lessy______than
Less than or equal to
Greatery______than
Greater than or equal to</td><td>L → R</td></tr>
<tr><td>8</td><td>Equality</td><td>==
!=</td><td>Equaly______to
Not Equal to</td><td>L → R</td></tr>
<tr><td>9</td><td>Bitwise AAND</td><td>&</td><td>Bitwise AND</td><td>L → R</td></tr>
<tr><td>10</td><td>Bitwise XOR</td><td>^</td><td>Bitwise XOR</td><td>L → R</td></tr>
<tr><td>11</td><td>Bitwise OR</td><td>|</td><td>Bitwise OR</td><td>L → R</td></tr>
<tr><td>12</td><td>Logical AND</td><td>&&</td><td>Logical AND</td><td>L → R</td></tr>
<tr><td>14</td><td>Conditional</td><td>? :</td><td>Ternary Operator</td><td>R → L</td></tr>
<tr><td>15</td><td>Assignment</td><td>=
*=
%=
/=
+=
-=
&=
^=
|=
<<=
>>=</td><td>Assignment
Assign product
Assign reminder
Assign quotient
Assign sum
Assign difference
Assign bitwise AND
Assign bitwise XOR
Assign bitwise OR
Assign left shift
Assign right shift</td><td>R → L</td></tr>
</table>

EXERCISE

(1) What is the effect of dividing an integer by a real quantity?
(2) How would you use the cast operator to convert(7*9/11) to double?
(3) What are unary operators?
(4) How many operands are associated with a unary operators?
(5) Describe the difference between increment and decrement operators.
(6) What is the associativity of unary operators?
(7) What is sizeof operator?
(8) What is the difference between = and == ?
(9) What logical operator negates the truth value of the expression to its immediate right?
(10) What integer value is equivalent to false?
(11) What is the associativity of logical NOT?
(12) What are the 6 assignment operators?
(13) How can multiple assignments be written in C?
(14) Define the associativity of conditional operators.

Summary Questions:

(1) What is an operator? Describe different types of operators?
(2) What is an operand? What is the relationship between operators & operands?
(3) Summarize the rules that apply to expression whose operands are of different type?
(4) When should parentheses be included within the expression?
(5) How can the conditional operator be combined with the assignment operator to form an "if-else" type statement?

(1) Which bit wise operator is suitable for checking whether a particular bit is on or off?
(2) Which bit wise operator is suitable for turning off a particular bit in a number?
(3) Which one is equivalent to multiplying by 2:Left shifting a number by 1 or Left shifting an unsigned int or char by 1?

Programs:

(1) How to add two numbers without using the plus operator?
(2) How to swap two numbers using bitwise operators?

Program 4.1

Adding two integers.c — Add two numbers and print them out together with their sum

```
#include <stdio.h>
int main(void)
  {
  int first, second;
  printf("Enter two integers > ");
  scanf("%d %d", &first, &second);
  printf("The two numbers are: %d  %d\n", first, second);
  printf("Their sum is %d\n", first+second);
  }
```

Program 4.2

FILE: Finding the value of a collection of coins.c * DETERMINES THE VALUE OF A COIN COLLECTION

```
#include <stdio.h>
void main ()
  {
/* Local data ... */
  int pennies;          // input: count of pennies
  int nickels;          // input: count of nickels
  int dimes;            // input: count of dimes
  int quarters;         // input: count of quarters
  int temp, left;       // temporaries for various
                        // computations
  /* Read in the count of quarters, dimes, nickels and pennies. */
  printf("Enter the number of quarters, dimes, nickels, and pennies: ");
  scanf("%d %d %d %d", &quarters, &dimes, &nickels, &pennies);
  /* Compute the total value in cents. */
  left = 25 * quarters + 10 * dimes + 5 * nickels + pennies;
  /* Find and display the value in dollars */
  printf("Your collection is worth\n ");
  temp = left / 100;
  printf("\t%d dollar", temp);
```

```
if (temp==1)
  printf(", ");
else
  printf("s, ");
left = left % 100;
/* Find and display the value left in quarters */
temp = left / 25;
printf("%d quarter", temp);
if (temp==1)
  printf(", ");
else
  printf("s, ");
left = left % 25;
/* Find and display the value left in dimes */
temp = left / 10;
printf("%d dime", temp);
/* Here, just for fun, instead of using a conditional statement,
I use a conditional expression and string concatenation*/
printf ((temp==1) ? ", " : "s, ");
left = left % 10;
/* Find and display the value left in nickels */
temp = left / 5;
printf("%d nickel", temp);
if (temp==1)
  printf(", and ");
else
  printf("s, and ");
left = left % 5;
/* Find and display the value left in pennies */
printf("%d penn", left);
if (left==1)
  printf("y\n");
else
  printf("ies\n");
}
```

5

Control Statements

Objective

In this chapter you will learn the use of control statements in C such as branching and looping statements

5.1 Introduction

Statements represent the lowest-level building blocks of a program. Statements are useful because of the side-effects they cause, the combination of which enables the program to serve a specific purpose. A running program spends all of its time executing statements. The order in which statements are executed is called control flow. Flow control in a program is typically sequential, from one statement to the next, but may be diverted to other paths by branch statements. Flow control is an important consideration because it determines what is executed during a run and what is not, therefore, affecting the overall outcome of the program. Like many other procedural languages, C provides different forms of statements for different purposes. Declaration statements are used for defining variables. Assignment-like statements are used for simple, algebraic computations. Branching statements are used for specifying alternate paths of execution, depending on the outcome of a logical condition. Loop statements are used for specifying computations which need to be repeated until a certain logical condition is satisfied. Flow control statements are used to divert the execution path to another part of the program.

5.2 Simple and Compound Statements

A simple statement is a computation terminated by a semicolon. Variable definitions and semicolon-terminated expressions are examples:

```
int i;                  // declaration statement
double d = 10.5; // declaration statement
```

The simplest statement is the null statement which consists of just a semicolon: ; // null statement. Multiple statements can be combined into a compound statement by enclosing them within braces. For example:

```
{
 int mark1=45,mark2=67,avgMarks
avgMarks= (mark1+mark2)/2
}
```

Compound statements are useful in two ways: (i) they allow us to put multiple statements in places where otherwise only single statements are allowed, and (ii) they allow us to introduce a new scope in the program. A scope is a part of the program text within which a variable remains defined. Because a compound statement may contain variable definitions and defines a scope for them, it is also called a block. The scope of a C variable is limited to the block immediately enclosing it. A program consists of a number of statements which are usually executed in sequence. Programs can be much more powerful if we can control the order in which statements are run.

5.2.1 Assignment: where values, usually the results of calculations, are stored in variables.

5.2.2 Control: the program makes a decision about what to do next. C provides two styles of flow control:

Branching

Looping

Branching is deciding what actions to take and looping is deciding how many times to take a certain action.

5.3 The if else Statement

This is used to decide whether to do something at a special point, or to decide between two courses of action. It takes an expression in parenthesis a statement or block of statements. if the expression is true then the statement or block of statements gets executed otherwise these statements are skipped.

The general syntax is as below :

```
if (expression)
  Statement;

or

if (expression)
{
  Block of statements;
}
```

or

```
if (expression)
{
  Block of statements;
}
else
{
  Block of statements;
}
```

If we wish to have more than one statement following if or the else, they should be grouped together between curly brackets. Such a grouping is called a compound statement or a block. Sometimes we wish to make a multi-way decision based on several conditions. The most general way of doing this is by using the else if variant on if statement. This works by cascading several comparisons. As soon as one of these gives a true result, the following statement or block is executed, and no further comparisons are performed.

```
if (expression)
{
  Block of statements;
}
else if(expression)
{
  Block of statements;
}
else
{
  Block of statements;
}
```

5.4 The Switch Statement

The switch statement provides a way of choosing between a set of alternatives, based on the value of an expression. The general form of the switch statement is:

```
switch (expression)
{
case constant1:
statements;
...
case constantn:
statements;
default:
statements;
}
```

First *expression* (called the switch tag) is evaluated, and the outcome is compared to each of the numeric *constant*s (called case labels), in the order they appear, until a match is found. The *statements* following the matching case are then executed. Note the plural: each case may be followed by zero or more statements (not just one statement). Execution continues until either a break statement is encountered or all intervening statements until the end of the switch statement are executed. The final default case is optional and is exercised if none of the earlier cases provide a match

5.5 Loops

The other main type of control statement is the loop. Loops allow a statement, or block of statements, to be repeated. Computers are very good at repeating simple tasks many times, the loop is C's way of achieving this C gives you a choice of three types of loop, *while, do while* and *for.*

5.5.1 While Loop

The while loop keeps repeating an action until an associated test returns false. This is useful where the programmer does not know in advance how many times the loop will be traversed.

The general syntax is as below:

```
while(Condition)
    {
    Block of statements
}
```

Example:

```
int string_length(char string[])
{     int i = 0;

      while (string[i] != '\0')
            i++;

      return(i);
}
```

The string is passed to the function as an argument. The size of the array is not specified, the function will work for a string of any size.The while loop is used to look at the characters in the string one at a time until the null character is found. Then the loop is exited and the index of the null is returned. While the character is not null, the index is incremented and the test is repeated.

5.5.2 Do While Loop

The do while loop is similar to while loop but the test occurs after the loop body is executed. This ensures that the loop body is run at least once before continuing. Such a setup is frequently used where data is to be read. The test then verifies the data, and loops back to read again if it was unacceptable.

The general syntax is as below:

```
do
{
Block of statements
}while (Condition)
```

Example:

```
do
{     printf("Enter 1 for yes, 0 for no :");
      scanf("%d", &input_value);
} while (input_value != 1 && input_value != 0);.
```

5.5.3 For Loop

The for loop is frequently used usually where the loop will be traversed a fixed number of times. It is very flexible, and novice programmers should take care not to abuse the power it offers.

The general syntax is as below:

```
for(Declaration/Initialization; Condition; Increment/Decrement)
{
Block of statements
}
```

The head of the loop consists of three parts separated by semicolons. The first is run before the loop is entered. This is usually the initialization of the loop variable. The second is a test, the loop is exited when this returns false. The third is a statement to be run every time the loop body is completed. This is usually an increment of the loop counter. However any of them can be left blank. A blank first or last statement will mean no initialization or running increment. A blank comparison statement will always be treated as true. This will cause the loop to run indefinitely unless interrupted by some other means. This might be a return or a break statement. It is also possible to squeeze several statements into the first or third position, separating them with commas. This allows a loop with more than one controlling variable.

Example:

```
float average(float array[], int count)
{       float total = 0.0;
        int i;

        for(i = 0; i < count; i++)
        total += array[i];

        return(total / count);
}
```

The other form of for loop are as below:

```
for(;Condition; Increment/Decrement)
    {
    Block of statements
    }
for(Declaration/Initialization;; Increment/Decrement)
    {
    Block of statements
    }
```

```
for (Declaration/Initalzation;Increment/Decrement;)
        {
        Block of statements
        }
for(;;)
        {
        Block of statements
        }
```

5.6 The Break Statement

We have already met break in the discussion of the switch statement. It is used to exit from a loop or a switch, control passing to the first statement beyond the loop or a switch. With loops, break can be used to force an early exit from the loop, or to implement a loop with a test to exit in the middle of the loop body.

5.7 The Continue Statement

This is similar to break but is encountered less frequently. It only works within loops where its effect is to force an immediate jump to the loop control statement.

In a while loop, jump to the test statement.

In a do while loop, jump to the test statement.

In a for loop, jump to the test, and perform the iteration.

5.8 The Goto Statement

The goto statement provides the lowest-level of jumping. It has the general form:

goto *label*;

where *label* is an identifier which marks the jump destination of goto. The label should be followed by a colon and appear before a statement within the same function as the goto statement itself. For example, the role of the break statement in the for loop in the previous section can be emulated by a goto:

```
for (i = 0; i < attempts; ++i) {
if (i%5==0 && i%7==0) goto out; /* drop out of the loop */
printf ("i = %d",i)
}
```

Because goto provides a free and unstructured form of jumping (unlike break and continue), it can be easily misused. It is strongly recommend, not to use goto. Nevertheless, goto does have some legitimate (though rare) uses.

EXERCISE

(1) Differentiate between a for loop and a while loop? What are it uses?

(2) What is difference between 'break' and 'continue' statements?

Programs:

(1) Write a C program To find the sum of individual digits of a given integer number.

(2) Write a C program to find the sum and average of a given array of integer numbers

(3) Write a C program to find the GCD and LCD of given two integer numbers .

(4) Write a C program to find the reverse of a given integer number .

(5) How to generate prime numbers? How to generate the next prime after a given prime?

(6) Write a C program which asks the user for a number between 1 to 9 and shows the number. If the user inputs a number out of the specified range,the program should show an error and prompt the user for a valid input.

(7) Write a program to display the multiplication table of a given number.

(8) Write a program to check whether a given number is even or odd.

(9) Write a program to find the greatest of three numbers.

(10) Write a program to check whether a given number is a prime.

(11) Write a program to find the greatest among ten numbers.

(12) Write a program to swap two numbers using a temporary variable.

(13) Write a program to swap two numbers without using

(14) How can we sum the digits of a given number in single statement?

(15) Write a C program to check for palindromes.

(16) Write a program to find the Factorial of a number.

(17) Write a program to generate the Fibonacci Series

(18) How to print a pattern as shown below?

```
1
2 3
4 5 6
7 8 9 10
```

(19) Write C program to print the following pattern:

```
    1
   2 2
  3 3 3
 4 4 4 4
5 5 5 5 5
```

(20) Write C program to print the following pattern:

```
        1
      1 2 1
    1 2 3 2 1
  1 2 3 4 3 2 1
1 2 3 4 5 4 3 2 1
```

(21) Write a C program to display the following format:

```
____
a b
____
1 5
2 4
3 3
4 2
5 1
____
```

(22) Write a C program to display the following format:

```
______
no. sum
______
1 1
2 3
3 6
4 10
5 15
```

Program 5.1

Computing powers of 2.c — Print out powers of 2: 1, 2, 4, 8, .. up to 2^N

```
#include <stdio.h>
#define N 10
int main(void)
  {
  int n;          /* The current exponent */
  int val = 1;    /* The current power of 2 */
  printf("\t n \t   2^n\n");
  printf("\t=================\n");
  for (n=0; n<=N; n++)
      {
      printf("\t%3d \t %6d\n", n, val);
      val = 2*val;
      }
  return 0;
  }
It prints out :
    n   2^n
  ==========
    0    1
    1     2
    2     4
    3     8
    4    16
    5    32
    6    64
    7   128
    8   256
    9   512
   10  1024
```

Program 5.2

Adding n integers.c — Read a positive number N. Then read N integers and print them out together with their sum.

```
#include <stdio.h>
int main(void)
  {
  int n;       /* The number of numbers to be read */
  int sum;     /* The sum of numbers already read  */
  int current; /* The number just read             */
  int lcv;     /* Loop control variable, it counts the number
                  of numbers already read */
   printf("Enter a positive number n > ");
  scanf("%d",&n); /* We should check that n is really positive
  sum = 0;
  for (lcv=0; lcv < n; lcv++)
      {
      printf("\nEnter an integer > ");
      scanf("%d",&current);
      printf("\nThe number was %d\n", current);
      sum = sum + current;
      }
  printf("The sum is %d\n", sum);
  return 0;
  }
```

Program 5.3

Adding a sequence of positive integers.c — Read a sequence of positive integers and print them out together with their sum. Use a Sentinel value (say 0) to determine when the sequence has terminated.

```
#include <stdio.h>
#define SENTINEL 0
int main(void)
  {
    int sum = 0; /* The sum of numbers already read */
    int current; /* The number just read */
    do
        {
        printf("\nEnter an integer > ");
        scanf("%d", &current);
        if (current > SENTINEL)
          sum = sum + current;
        } while (current > SENTINEL);
    printf("\nThe sum is %d\n", sum);
      }
```

Program 5.4

Determining if a number is a prime.c It prompts the user to enter an integer N. It prints out if it is a prime or not. If not, it prints out a factor of N.

```
#include <stdio.h>
int main(void)
  {
    int n, i;
    int flag;
    printf("Enter value of N > ");
    scanf("%d", &n);
    flag = 1;
    for (i=2; (i<(n/2)) && flag; )
      { /* May be we do not need to test
```

```
            values of i greater than the square root of n? */
            if ((n % i) == 0) /* If true n is divisible by i */
            flag = 0;
            else
            i++;
        }
    if (flag)
    printf("%d is prime\n", n);
    else
    printf("%d has %d as a factor\n", n, i);
    return 0;
    }
```

Program 5.5

Finding all the proper factors of a number.c — It prompts the user to enter an integer N. It prints out if it is a prime or not. If not, it prints out all of its proper factors.

```
#include <stdio.h>
int main(void)
    {
    int n,
    lcv,
  flag; /* flag initially is 1 and becomes 0 if we determine that n
        is not a prime */
    printf("Enter value of N > ");
    scanf("%d", &n);
    for (lcv=2, flag=1; lcv <= (n / 2); lcv++)
        {
        if ((n % lcv) == 0)
            {
            if (flag)
            printf("The non-trivial factors of %d are: \n", n);
            flag = 0;
            printf("\t%d\n", lcv);
            }
        }
    if (flag)
    printf("%d is prime\n", n);
    }
```

Program 5.6

Computing Fibonacci numbers.c — It prints out the first N Fibonacci * numbers.

```
#include <stdio.h>
int main(void)
   {
   int n;        /* The number of Fibonacci numbers we will print */
   int i;        /* The index of Fibonacci number to be printed next */
   int current;  /* The value of the (i)th Fibonacci number */
   int next;     /* The value of the (i+1)th Fibonacci number */
   int twoaway;  /* The value of the (i+2)th Fibonacci number */
   printf("How many Fibonacci numbers do you want to compute? ");
   scanf("%d", &n);
   if (n<=0)
   printf("The number should be positive.\n");
   else
      {
      printf("\n\n\tI \t Fibonacci(I) \n\t==========\n");
      next = current = 1;
      for (i=1; i<=n; i++)
         {
         printf("\t%d \t   %d\n", i, current);
         twoaway = current+next;
         current = next;
         next    = twoaway;
         }
      }
   }
```

The output from a run of this program was:

```
How many Fibonacci numbers do you want to compute? 9
   I   Fibonacci(I)
   ================
   1   1
   2   1
   3   2
   4   3
   5   5
   6   8
   7   13
   8   21
   9   34
```

PART – II

6

PREPROCESSOR

OBJECTIVE

In this chapter you will learn The Preprocessor, Preprocessor directives, Macros, #define identifier string, Simple macro substitution, Macros as arguments, Nesting of macros, Undefining a macro and File inclusion

6.1 Introduction

A unique feature of C language is the preprocessor. A programmer can use the tools provided by preprocessor to make his program easy to read, modify, portable and more efficient. Preprocessor is a program that processes the code before it passes through the compiler. It operates under the control of preprocessor command lines and directives. Preprocessor directives are placed in the source program before the main line. Before the source code passes through the compiler, it is examined by the preprocessor for any preprocessor directives. If there is any, appropriate actions are taken then the source program is handed over to the compiler. Preprocessor directives follow the special syntax rules and begin with the symbol #in column1 and do not require any semicolon at the end. A set of commonly used preprocessor directives are as follows:

6.2 Preprocessor Directives

Directive	Function
#define	Defines a macro substitution
#undef	Undefines a macro
#include	Specifies a file to be included
#ifdef	Tests for macro definition
#endif	Specifies the end of #if
#ifndef	Tests whether the macro is not def
#if	Tests a compile time condition
#else	Specifies alternatives when # if test fails

The preprocessor directives can be divided into three categories

(1) Macro substitution division

(2) File inclusion division

(3) Compiler control division

6.3 Macros

Macro substitution is a process where an identifier in a program is replaced by a pre defined string composed of one or more tokens. We can use the #define statement for the task. It has the following form

#define identifier string

The preprocessor replaces every occurrence of the identifier in the source code by the string. The definition should start with the keyword #define and should follow with identifier and a string with at least one blank space between them. The string may be any text and identifier must be a valid c name.

There are different forms of macro substitution. The most common form is:

(1) Simple macro substitution

(2) Argument macro substitution

(3) Nested macro substitution

Simple macro substitution:

Simple string replacement is commonly used to define constants. Example:

```
#define pi 3.1415926
```

Writing macro definition in capitals is a convention not a rule. A macro definition can include more than a simple constant value. It can include expressions as well. Following is valid example:

```
#define AREA 12.36
```

Macro as arguments:

The preprocessor permits us to define more complex and more useful form of replacements. It takes the following form.

```
# define identifier(f1,f2,f3.....fn) string.
```

Notice that there is no space between identifier and left parentheses and the identifier f1,f2,f3 .... Fn is analogous to formal arguments in a function definition.

There is a basic difference between simple replacement discussed above and replacement of macro arguments. It is known as a macro call:

A simple example of a macro with arguments is

```
# define CUBE (x) (x*x*x)
```

If the following statements appears later in the program,

volume=CUBE(side);

The preprocessor would expand the statement to

volume =(side*side*side)

Nesting of macros:

We can also use one macro in the definition of another macro. That is macro definitions may be nested. Consider the following macro definition

```
# define SQUARE(x)((x)*(x))
```

Undefining a macro:

A defined macro can be undefined using the statement

```
# undef identifier.
```

This is useful when we want to restrict the definition only to a particular part of the program.

File inclusion:

The preprocessor directive "#include file name" can be used to include any file in to your program if the functions or macro definitions are present in an external file they can be included in your file In the directive the filename is the name of the file containing the required definitions or functions alternatively. This directive can take the form

```
#include< filename >
```

Without double quotation marks. In this format the file will be searched in only standard directories. The c preprocessor also supports a more general form of test condition #if directive. This takes the following form :

```
#if constant expression
{
statement-1;
statement-2'
....
....
}
#endif
```

the constant expression can be a logical expression such as test < = 3 etc

If the result of the constant expression is true then all the statements between the #if and #endif are included for processing otherwise they are skipped. The names TEST LEVEL etc., may be defined as macros.

■ ■ ■

7

INPUT AND OUTPUT

OBJECTIVE

In this chapter you will learn about single character input output, String input and output, Formatted Input For Scanf, Input specifications for real number, Input specifications for a character, Printing One Line, Conversion Strings and Specifiers, Specifier Meaning.

7.1 Introduction

When you take time to consider it, a computer would be pretty useless without some way to talk to the people who use it. Just like we need information in order to accomplish tasks, so do computers. And just as we supply information to others so that *they* can do tasks, so do computers. These supplies and returns of information to a computer are called input and output. 'Input' is information supplied to a computer or program. 'Output' is information provided by a computer or program. Frequently, computer programmers will lump the discussion in the more general term *input/output* or simply, I/O. In most of the C programs the reading and writing of data will be done through the terminal, disk files or database files. In this chapter we cover how input and output is performed using the standard keyboard and terminal as the I/O devices. There are many different ways for a program to communicate with the user. Amazingly, the simplest methods usually taught to beginning programmers may also be the most powerful. In the "Hello World" example at the beginning of this text, we were introduced to a Standard Library file stdio.h, and one of its functions, printf(). Here we discuss more of the functions that stdio.h gives us.

7.2 Single Character Input Output

The basic operation done in input output is to read a character from the standard input device such as the keyboard and to output or writing it to the output unit usually the screen. The getchar() function can be used to read a character from the standard input device. The scanf can also be used to achieve the function.

getchar() :

The getchar() has the following form.

Variable_name = getchar():

Variable name is a valid 'C' variable, that has been declared already and that possess the type char.

putchar() :

The putchar() function which in analogous to getchar() function can be used for writing characters one at a time to the output terminal. The general form is

putchar(Variable_name);

Displays the value stored in variable c to the standard screen.

7.3 String Input and Output

The gets() function receives the string from standard input device while puts() outputs the string to the standard output device. A string is an array or set of characters. The function gets() accepts the name of the string as a parameter, and fills the string with characters that are input from the keyboard till newline character is encountered. At the end function appends a null terminator as must be done to any string and returns. The puts() function displays the contents stored in its parameter on the standard screen.

gets() :

The standard form of the gets function is

gets(str) /* str is a string variable. */

puts() :

The standard form for the puts character is

puts(str) /* str is a string variable. */

7.4 Formatted Input for Scanf

7.4.1 scanf()

The formatted input refers to input data that has been arranged in a particular format. Input values are generally taken by using the scanf function.

The scanf function has the general form.

```
scanf ("control string", arg1, arg2, arg3 ............argn);
```

The format field is specified by the control string and the arguments arg1, arg2, ...argn specifies the address of location where address is to be stored. The control string specifies the field format which includes format specifications and optional number specifying field width and the conversion character % and also blanks, tabs and newlines. The Blanks tabs and newlines are ignored by compiler. The conversion character % is followed by the type of data that is to be assigned to variable of the assignment. The field width Specifier is optional.

A simple program to illustrate the use of scanf statement:-

```
#include <stdio.h>
char name[20];
int main(void)
{
 scanf("%s",&name);
 return 0;
}
```

7.4.2 printf()

The most simple output statement can be produced in C' Language by using printf statement. It allows you to display information required to the user and also print the variables. We can also format the output and provide text labels.

The simple statement such as

printf ("Enter 2 numbers");

Prompts the message enclosed in the quotation to be displayed.

A simple program to illustrate the use of printf statement:-

```
#include <stdio.h>
int main(void)
{
 printf("Hello, world!\n");
 return 0;
}
```

Conversion Strings and Specifiers:

The printf ( ) function is quite flexible. It allows a variable, number of arguments, labels and sophisticated formatting of output.

The general form of the printf ( ) function is

```
printf ("conversion string", variable list);
```

The conversion string includes all the text labels, escape character and conversion specifiers required for the desired output. The variable includes all the variable to be printed in order they are to be printed. There must be a conversion specified for each variable.

7.5 Printing Numbers and Escape Sequences

The printf function is a powerful function, and is probably the most-used function in C programs.

```
#include <stdio.h> /* this is important, since printf
                cannot be used without this line */
int main(void)
{
  printf("1905+31214 is");
  return 0;
}
```

printf() has methods for printing numbers. What we do is put a *placeholder* format code in the string. We write: printf("1905+31214 is %d", 1905+31214);

The placeholder %d literally "holds the place" for the actual number that is the result of adding 1905 to 31214.These placeholders are called format Specifiers.

7.6 Specifier Meaning

%c – Print a character
%d – Print a Integer
%i – Print a Integer
%e – Print float value in exponential form.
%f – Print float value
%g – Print using %e or %f whichever is smaller
%o – Print actual value
%s – Print a string
%x – Print a hexadecimal integer (Unsigned) using lower case a – F
%X – Print a hexadecimal integer (Unsigned) using upper case A – F
%a – Print a unsigned integer.
%p – Print a pointer value
%hx – hex short
%lo – octal long
%ld – long

Examples:

A program asking the user to enter two numbers and then display their sum:

```
#include <stdio.h>
int main(void)
{
 int number1, number2;
 printf("Please input an integer value: ");
 scanf("%d", &number1);
 printf("Please input an integer value: ");
 scanf("%d", &number2);
 printf("%d + %d = %d\n", number1, number2, number1 + number2);
 return 0;
}
```

EXERCISE

(1) What function does C use for I/O operations?

(2) What header file does getchar() and putchar() need?

(3) Do printf() and scanf() require some header file?

(4) How does getchar() work?

(5) When does getchar() stop reading characters from the standard input?

(6) What generates an EOF on MS-DOS system?

(7) How does putchar() work?

(8) What is a commonly used formatted output statement in C?

(9) What parameters are needed to use a printf() function?

(10) If int salary=9; then how would you print the following statement on the screen "Your salary is 9" ?

(11) What does %d stand for ?

(12) What does %s stand for ?

(13) What does %f stand for ?

(14) When do we need scanf()?

(15) What does scanf() require to read a variable from the standard input?

(16) What does name of an array also mean?

(17) How different are gets() and puts() from printf() and scanf()?

(18) How does gets() work?

(19) How does puts() work?

(20) How would you ask a user his name on the screen using puts() and how would you read the answer given by the user using gets()?

Program 7.1

line.c — It reads lines from input and echos them back.

```
#include <stdio.h>
int main(void)
    {
    char c;
    int count;
    for(;;)
        {
        count=0;
        printf("Please enter a line [blank line to terminate]> ");
            do{
                c=getchar();
                putchar(c);
                count++;
            }while (c!='\n');
            if(count==1)break;
        }
    }
```

■■■

8

FUNCTIONS

OBJECTIVE

In this chapter you will learn Function definition, Structure of a Function, use of Functions, Function Declaration, Calling the Function, Function Definition, The general guideline for the function, Types Of Functions, Void Functions, Call By Value, Call By Reference, Recursion, The Scope And Lifetime Of Variables , String Operations

8.1 What is a Function?

A function is a complete and independent program which is used (or invoked) by the main program or other subprograms. A subprogram receives values called arguments from a calling program, performs calculations and returns the results to the calling program.

There are many advantages in using functions in a program they are:

(1) It facilitates top down modular programming. In this programming style, the high level logic of the overall problem is solved first while the details of each lower level functions is addressed later.

(2) the length of the source program can be reduced by using functions at appropriate places. This factor is critical with microcomputers where memory space is limited.

(3) It is easy to locate and isolate a faulty function for further investigation.

(4) A function may be used by many other programs this means that a C programmer can build on what others have already done, instead of starting over from scratch.

(5) A program can be used to avoid rewriting the same sequence of code at two or more locations in a program. This is especially useful if the code involved is long or complicated.

(6) Programming teams does a large percentage of programming. If the program is divided into subprograms, each subprogram can be written by one or two team members of the team rather than having the whole team to work on the complex program.

We can divide a long C program into small blocks which can perform a certain task. A function is a self contained block of statements that perform a coherent task of same kind.

8.2 Structure of a Function

There are two main parts of the function. The function header and the function body.

```
int sum(int x, int y)
{
    int ans = 0;        //holds the answer that will be returned
    ans = x + y;        //calculate the sum
    return ans          //return the answer
}
```

8.2.1 Function Header

In the first line of the above code

int sum(int x, int y)

It has three main parts

(1) The name of the function, i.e., sum

(2) The parameters of the function enclosed in paranthesis

(3) Return value type, i.e., int

8.2.2 Function Body

Whatever is written with in { } in the above example is the body of the function.

8.2.3 Function Prototypes

The prototype of a function provides the basic information about a function which tells the compiler that the function is used correctly or not. It contains the same information as the function header contains.

The prototype of the function in the above example would be like

int sum (int x, int y);

The only difference between the header and the prototype is the semicolon ; there must be a semicolon at the end of the prototype.

8.3 Why we use Functions

The most important reason to use functions is to aid in the conceptual organization of a program. The function"s code is stored in only one place in memory, even though the function is executed many times in the course of the program. Some reasons are given below

(1) Many programs require that a specific function is repeated many times instead of writing the function code as many times as it is required we can write it as a single function and access the same function again and again as many times as it is required.

(2) We can avoid writing redundant program code of some instructions again and again.

(3) Programs with using functions are compact & easy to understand.

(4) Testing and correcting errors is easy because errors are localized and corrected.

(5) We can understand the flow of program, and its code easily since the readability is enhanced while using the functions.

(6) A single function written in a program can also be used in other programs also.

8.4 Function Declaration

Just as you cant use a variable without first telling the compiler what it is, you also cannot use a functions without telling the compiler about it, There are two ways to do this. The approach we show here is to declare the function before it is called. The other approach is to define it before it is called; we will examine that next. In the Table program, the functions starline() is declared in the line.

void starline ( );

The declaration tells the compiler that at some later point we plan to present a function called starline. The keyword void specifies that the function has no return value, and the empty parentheses indicate that it takes no arguments. Notice that the function declarations is terminated with a semicolon It is a complete statement in itself. Function declarations are also called prototypes, since they provide a model or blueprint for the function. They tell the compiler," a function that looks like this is coming up later in the program, so it is all right if you see references to it before you see the function itself."

8.5 Calling the Function

The function is called (or invoked) three times from main (). Each of the three calls look like this:

starline():

This is all we need to call a function name, followed by parentheses. The syntax of the call is very similar to that of declaration, except that the return type is not used. A semicolon terminates the call. Executing the call statement causes the function to execute; that is, control is transferred to the function, the statement in the function definition are executed, and then control returns to the statement following the function call.

8.6 Function Definition

Finally, we come to the functions itself, which is referred to as the function's definition, The definition contains the actual code for the function. Here's the definition for starline().

```
void starline ( )
{
for ( intj=0, j < 45; j++ )
cout << "*" ;
cout << endl;
}
```

The definition consists of a line called the decelerator, followed by the function body. The function body is composed of the statements that make up the function, delimited by braces.

The decelerator must agree with the declaration: It must use the same function name, have the same argument types in the same order (if there are arguments), and have the same return type. Notice that a semicolon does not terminate the declarator. When the function is called, control is transferred to the first statement in the functions body. The other statements in the function body are then executed, and when the closing brace is encountered, control returns to the calling program.

There are basically two types of functions

Library functions Ex. printf ( ), scanf ( ) etc.

User defined function

```
main ( )
{
message ( );
}
```

8.7 The General Guideline for the Function

Function is defined when function name is followed by a pair of braces in which one or more statements may be present for, e.g.,

```
message ( )
{
statement 1;
statement 2;
statement 3;
}
```

(1) Any function can be called from any other function even main ( ) can be called from other functions for, e.g.,

```
main ( )
{
message ( );
}
message ( )
{
printf (" \n Hello");
main ( );
}
```

(2) A function can be called any number of times for, e.g.,

```
main ()
{
message ( );
message ( );
}
message ( )
{
printf ("\n Hello");
}
```

(3) The order in which the functions are defined in a program and the order in which they get called need not necessarily be same for, e.g.,

```
main ( );
{
message 1 ( );
message 2 ( );
}
message 2 ( )
{
printf ("\n I am learning C");
}
message 1 ( )
{
printf ( "\n Hello ");
}
```

(4) A function can call itself, such a process is called "recursion".

(5) A function can be called from other function, but a function cannot be defined in another function. These the following program code would be wrong, since Argentina is being defined inside another function main ( ).

```
main ( )
{
printf ("\n I am in main");
argentina ( )
{
printf {"\n I am in argentina");
}
}
```

(6) Any C program contains at least one function.

(7) If a program contains only one function, it must be main( ).

(8) In a C program if there are more than one functional present then one of these functional must be main( ) because program execution always begins with main( ).

(9) There is no limit on the number of functions that might be present in a C program.

(10) Each function in a program is called in the sequence specified by the function calls in main( )

(11) After each function has done its thing, control returns to the main( ), when main( ) runs out of function calls, the program ends.

Functions declaration and prototypes of any function by default returns an int value. If we desire that a function should return a value other than an int, then it is necessary to explicitly mention so in the calling functions as well as in the called function for, e.g.,

```
main ( )
 {
 float a,b,
 printf ("\n Enter any number");
 scanf ("\% f", &a );
 b = square (a)
 printf ("\n square of % f is % f", a,b);
 }
 square (float X)
 {
 float y;
 Y = x * x;
 return (y);
}
```

the sample run of this program is Enter any number 2.5 square of 2.5 is 6.000000 Here 6 is not a square of 2.5 this happened because any C function, by default, always returns an integer value. The following program segment illustrates how to make square ( ) capable of returning a float value.

```
main ( )
   {
   float square ( );
   float a, b;
   printf ("\n Enter any number ");
   scanf ("%f" &a);
   b = square (a);
   printf ("\n square of % f is % f, " a,
   b);
   }
   float square (float x)
   {
   float y;
   y= x *x;
   return ( y);
  }
```

sample run Enter any number 2.5 square of 2.5 is 6.2500000

8.8 Types of Functions

A function may belong to any one of the following categories:

(1) Functions with no arguments and no return values.

(2) Functions with arguments and no return values.

(3) Functions with arguments and return values.

8.8.1 Functions with no arguments and no return values

Let us consider the following program

```
/* Program to illustrate a function with no argument and no return values*/
#include
main()
{
statement1();
starline();
statement2();
starline();
}
/*function to print a message*/
statement1()
{
printf("\n Sample subprogram output");
}
statement2()
{
printf("\n Sample subprogram output two");
}
starline()
{
int a;
for (a=1;a<60;a++)
printf("%c",'*');
printf("\n");
}
```

In the above example there is no data transfer between the calling function and the called function. When a function has no arguments it does not receive any data from the calling function. Similarly when it does not return value the calling function does not receive any data from the called function. A function that does not return any value cannot be used in an expression it can be used only as independent statement.

8.8.2 Functions with arguments but no return values

The nature of data communication between the calling function and the arguments to the called function and the called function does not return any values to the calling function this shown in example below:

Consider the following:

Function calls containing appropriate arguments. For example the function call

value (500,0.12,5)

Would send the values 500,0.12 and 5 to the function value (p, r, n) and assign values 500 to p, 0.12 to r and 5 to n. the values 500,0.12 and 5 are the actual arguments which become the values of the formal arguments inside the called function. Both the arguments actual and formal should match in number type and order. The values of actual arguments are assigned to formal arguments on a one to one basis starting with the first argument as shown below:

```
main()
{
function1(a1,a2,a3......an)
}

function1(f1,f2,f3....fn);
{
function body;
}
```

here a1,a2,a3 are actual arguments and f1,f2,f3 are formal arguments.

The no of formal arguments and actual arguments must be matching to each other suppose if actual arguments are more than the formal arguments, the extra actual arguments are discarded. If the number of actual arguments are less than the formal arguments then the unmatched formal arguments are initialized to some garbage values. In both cases no error message will be generated. The formal arguments may be valid variable names, the actual arguments may be variable names expressions or constants. The values used in actual arguments must be assigned values before the function call is made. When a function call is made only a copy of the values actual arguments is passed to the called function. What occurs inside the functions will have no effect on the variables used in the actual argument list.

Let us consider the following program

```
/*Program to find the largest of two numbers using function*/
#include
main()
{
int a,b;
printf("Enter the two numbers");
scanf("%d%d",&a,&b);
```

```
largest(a,b)
}
/*Function to find the largest of two numbers*/
largest(int a, int b)
{
if(a>b)
printf("Largest element=%d",a);
else
printf("Largest element=%d",b);
}
```

in the above program we could make the calling function to read the data from the terminal and pass it on to the called function. But function does not return any value.

8.8.3 Functions with arguments and return values

The function of the type arguments with return values will send arguments from the calling function to the called function and expects the result to be returned back from the called function back to the calling function. To assure a high degree of portability between programs a function should generally be coded without involving any input output operations. For example different programs may require different output formats for displaying the results. These shortcomings can be overcome by handing over the result of a function to its caliing function where the returned value can be used as required by the program. In the above type of function the following steps are carried out:

(1) The function call transfers the controls along with copies of the values of the actual arguments of the particular function where the formal arguments are created and assigned memory space and are given the values of the actual arguments.

(2) The called function is executed line by line in normal fashion until the return statement is encountered. The return value is passed back to the function call is called function.

(3) The calling statement is executed normally and return value is thus assigned to the calling function.

Note that the value return by any function when no format is specified is an integer.

8.8.4 Return value data type of function

A C function returns a value of type int as the default data type when no other type is specified explicitly. For example if function does all the calculations by using float values and if the return statement such as return (sum); returns only the integer part of the sum. This is since we have not specified any return type for the sum. There is the necessity in some cases it is important to receive float or character or double data type. To enable a calling function to receive a non-integer value from a called function we can do the two things:

(1) The explicit type specifier corresponding to the data type required must be mentioned in the function header. The general form of the function definition is

```
Type_specifier function_name(argument list)
Argument declaration;
{
function statement;
}
```

The type specifier tells the compiler, the type of data the function is to return.

2. The called function must be declared at the start of the body in the calling function, like any other variable. This is to tell the calling function the type of data the function is actually returning. The program given below illustrates the transfer of a floating-point value between functions done in a multiple function program.

```
main()
{
float x,y,add();
double sub(0;
x=12.345;
y=9.82;
printf("%f\n" add(x,y));
printf("%lf\n"sub(x,y);
}
float add(a,b)
float a,b;
{
return(a+b);
}
double sub(p,q)
double p,q;
{
return(p-q);
}
```

We can notice that the functions too are declared along with the variables. These declarations clarify to the compiler that the return type of the function add is float and sub is double.

8.9 Void Functions

The functions that do not return any values can be explicitly defined as void. This prevents any accidental use of these functions in expressions.

```
main()
{
void starline();
void message();
______
}
void printline
{
statements;
}
void value
{
statements;
}
```

8.10 Call By Value

In the preceding examples we have seen that whenever we called a function we have always passed the values of variables to the called function. Such function calls are called "calls by value" by this what it meant is that on calling a function we are passing values of variables to it. The example of call by value are shown below ;

sum = calsum (a, b, c); f = factr (a);

In this method the value of each of the actual arguments in the calling function is copied into corresponding formal arguments of the called function. With this method the changes made to the formal arguments in the called function have no effect on the values of actual argument in the calling function. The following program illustrates this:

```
main ( )
{
int a = 10, b=20;
swapy (a,b);
printf ("\na = % d b = % d", a,b);
}
```

```
swapy (int x, int y)
{
int t;
t = x;
x = y;
y = t;
printf ( "\n x = % d y = % d" , x, y);
}
```

The output of the above program would be; x = 20 y = 10 a =10 b =20

8.11 Call By Reference (Read chapter pointer)

In the second method the addresses of actual arguments in the calling function are copied in to formal arguments of the called function. This means that using these addresses we would have an access to the actual arguments and hence we would be able to manipulate them the following program illustrates this.

```
main ( )
{
int a = 10, b =20,
swapv (&a, &b);
printf ("\n a = %d b= %d", a, b);
}
swapr (int **, int * y)
{
int t;
t = *x
*x = *y;
*y = t;
}
```

The output of the above program would be a = 20 b =10

8.12 Recursion

A recursive function is one which calls itself. This is another complicated idea which you are unlikely to meet frequently. We shall provide some examples to illustrate recursive functions. Recursive functions are useful in evaluating certain types of mathematical function. You may also encounter certain dynamic data structures such as linked lists or binary trees. Recursion is a very useful way of creating and accessing these structures.

Here is a recursive version of the Fibonacci function. We saw a non recursive version of this earlier.

```
int fib(int num)
/* Fibonacci value of a number */
{       switch(num) {
        case 0:
                return(0);
                break;
        case 1:
                return(1);
                break;
        default:  /* Including recursive calls */
                return(fib(num - 1) + fib(num - 2));
                break;
        }
}
```

We met another function earlier called power. Here is an alternative recursive version.

```
double power(double val, unsigned pow)
{
        if(pow == 0)  /* pow(x, 0) returns 1 */
                return(1.0);
        else
                return(power(val, pow - 1) * val);
}
```

Notice that each of these definitions incorporate a test. Where an input value gives a trivial result, it is returned directly, otherwise the function calls itself, passing a changed version of the input values. Care must be taken to define functions which will not call themselves indefinitely, otherwise your program will never finish. The definition of fib is interesting, because it calls itself twice when recursion is used. Consider the effect on program performance of such a function calculating the Fibonacci function of a moderate size number.

The another example of addition of parameters

```
#include <stdio.h>
int add(int k,int m);
main()
{
   int k ,i,m;
   m=2;
   k=3;
   i=add(k,m);
   printf("The value of addition is %d\n",i);
}
int add(int pk,int pm)
{
   if(pm==0)
      return(pk);
   else
      return(1+add(pk,pm-1));
}
The value of addition is 5
```

8.13 The Scope and Lifetime of Variables in Functions

The scope and lifetime of the variables define in C is not same when compared to other languages. The scope and lifetime depends on the storage class of the variable in C language the variables can be any one of the four storage classes:

(1) Automatic Variables

(2) External variable

(3) Static variable

(4) Register variable.

The scope actually determines over which part or parts of the program the variable is available. The lifetime of the variable retains a given value. During the execution of the program. Variables can also be categorized as local or global. Local variables are the variables that are declared within that function and are accessible to all the functions in a program and they can be declared within a function or outside the function also.

8.13.1 Automatic variables

Automatic variables are declared inside a particular function and they are created when the function is called and destroyed when the function exits. Automatic variables are local or private to a function in which they are defined by default all variable declared without any storage specification is automatic. The values of variable remains unchanged to the changes that may happen in other functions in the same program and by doing this no error occurs.

```
/* A program to illustrate the working of auto variables*/
#include
void main()
{
int m=1000;
function2();
printf("%d\n",m);
}

function1()
{
int m=10;
printf("%d\n",m);
}
function2()
{
int m=100;
function1();
printf("%d\n",m);
}
```

A local variable lives throughout the whole program although it accessible only in the main. A program with two subprograms function1 and function2 with m as automatic variable and is initialized to 10,100,1000 in function1, function2 and function3 respectively. When executed, main calls function2 which in turns calls function1. When main is active m=1000. But when function2 is called, the main m is temporarily put on the shelf and the new local m=100 becomes active. Similarly when function1 is called both previous values of m are put on shelf and latest value (m=10) become active, a soon as it is done main (m=1000) takes over. The output clearly shows that value assigned to m in one function does not affect its value in the other function. The local value of m is destroyed when it leaves a function.

8.13.2 External variables

Variables which are common to all functions and accessible by all functions of a program are internal variables. External variables can be declared outside a function.

Example:

```
int sum;
float percentage;
main()
{
.....
.....
}
function2()
{
....
....
}
```

The variables sum and percentage are available for use in all the three functions main, function1, function2. Local variables take precedence over global variables of the same name.

For example:

```
int i = 10;
void example(data)
int data;
{
int i = data;
}
main()
{
example(45);
}
```

In the above example both the global variable and local variable have the same name as i. The local variable i take precedence over the global variable. Also the value that is stored in integer i is lost as soon as the function exits.

A global value can be used in any function. All the functions in a program can access the global variable and change its value, the subsequent functions get the new value of the global variable, it will be inconvenient to use a variable as global because of this factor every function can change the value of the variable on its own and it will be difficult to get back the original value of the variable if it is required.

Global variables are usually declared in the beginning of the main program, i.e., before the main program however C provides a facility to declare any variable as global this is possible by using the keyword storage class extern. Although a variable has been defined after many functions the external declaration of y inside the function informs the compiler that the variable y is integer type defined somewhere else in the program. The external declaration does not allocate storage space for the variables. In case of arrays the definition should include their size as well. When a variable is defined inside a function as extern it provides type information only for that function. If it has to be used in other functions then again it has to be re-declared in that function also.

Example:

```
main()
{
int n;
out_put();
extern float salary[];
......
.....
out_put();
}
void out_put()
{
extern float salary[];
int n;
....
.....
}
float salary[size];
```

A function when its parameters and function body are specified this tells the compiler to allocate space for the function code and provides type info for the parameters. Since functions are external by default we declare them (in calling functions) without the qualifier extern.

8.13.3 Static variables

The value given to a variable declared by using keyword static persists until the end of the program. A static variable is initialized only once, when the program is compiled. It is never initialized again. During the first call to stat in the example shown below x is incremented to 1. because x is static, this value persists and therefore the next call adds another 1 to x giving it a value of 2. The value of x becomes 3 when third call is made. If we had declared x as an auto then output would here been x=1 all the three times.

```
main()
{
int j;
for(j=1;j&lt;3;j++)
stat();
}
stat();
{
static int x=0;
x=x+1;
printf("x=%d\n",x);
}
```

8.13.4 Register variables

A variable is usually stored in the memory but it is also possible to store a varible in the compilers register by defining it as register variable. The registers access is much faster than a memory access, keeping the frequently accessed variables in the register will make the execution of the program faster.

This is done as follows:

```
register int count;
```

Since only a few variables can be placed in a register, it is important to carefully select the variables for this purpose. However C will automatically convert register variables into normal variables once the limit is exceeded.

8.14 String Operations (string.h)

C language recognizes that string is a different class of array by letting us input and output the array as a unit and are terminated by null character. C library supports a large number of string handling functions that can be used to array out many of the string manipulations such as:

- Length (number of characters in the string)
- Concatentation (adding two are more strings)
- Comparing two strings
- Substring (Extract substring from a given string)
- Copy (copies one string over another).

To do all the operations described here it is essential to include string.h library header file in the program.

strlen() function:

This function counts and returns the number of characters in a string. The length does not include a null character.

Syntax n=strlen(string);

Where n is integer variable. Which receives the value of length of the string.

Example

length=strlen("Hollywood");

The function will assign number of characters 9 in the string to a integer variable length.

/*write a c program to find the length of the string using strlen() function*/

```
#include < stdio.h >
include < string.h >
void main()
{
char name[100];
int length;
printf("Enter the string");
gets(name);
length=strlen(name);
printf("\nNumber of characters in the string is=%d",length);
}
```

strcat() function:

when you combine two strings, you add the characters of one string to the end of other string. This process is called concatenation. The strcat() function joins 2 strings together. It takes the following form

```
strcat(string1,string2)
```

string1 & string2 are character arrays. When the function strcat is executed string2 is appended to string1. the string at string2 remains unchanged.

Example

strcpy(string1,"SIMCA");

strcpy(string2,"mca");

Printf("%s",strcat(string1,string2);

From the above program segment the value of string1 becomes *SIMCAmca*. The string at str2 remains unchanged as *mca*

strcmp function:

In c you cannot directly compare the value of 2 strings in a condition like if(string1==string2)

Most libraries however contain the strcmp() function, which returns a zero if 2 strings are equal, or a non zero number if the strings are not the same. The syntax of strcmp() is given below:

```
strcmp(string1,string2)
```

String1 & string2 may be string variables or string constants. String1, & string2 may be string variables or string constants some computers return a negative if the string1 is alphabetically less than the second and a positive number if the string is greater than the second.

Example:

strcmp("Pune","Pune") will return zero because 2 strings are equal.

strcmp("their","there") will return a 9 which is the numeric difference between ASCII 'i' and ASCII 'r'.

strcmp("The", "the") will return 32 which is the numeric difference between ASCII "T" & ASCII "t".

strcmpi() function

This function is same as strcmp() which compares 2 strings but not case sensitive.

Example

strcmpi("THE","the"); will return 0.

strcpy() function:

C does not allow you to assign the characters to a string directly as in the statement name="Hanmant";

Instead use the strcpy(0 function found in most compilers the syntax of the function is illustrated below.

```
strcpy(string1,string2);
```

Strcpy function assigns the contents of string2 to string1. string2 may be a character array variable or a string constant.

```
strcpy(name,"Sachin");
```

In the above example Sachin is assigned to the string called name.

strlwr () function:

This function converts all characters in a string from uppercase to lowercase.

syntax

```
strlwr(string);
```

For example:

strlwr("KADAM") converts to kadam.

strrev() function:

This function reverses the characters in a string.

Syntax

```
strrev(string);
```

For ex strrev("program") reverses the characters in a string into "margrop".

strupr() function:

This function converts all characters in a string from lower case to uppercase.

Syntax

```
strupr(string);
```

For example strupr("kadam") will convert the string to KADAM.

Program 8.1

```
/* Example program to use string functions*/
#include < stdio.h >
#include < string.h >
void main()
{
char s1[20],s2[20],s3[20];
int x,l1,l2,l3;
printf("Enter the strings");
scanf("%s%s",s1,s2);
x=strcmp(s1,s2);
if(x!=0)
    {
    printf("\nStrings are not equal\n");
    strcat(s1,s2);
            }
     else
        printf("\nStrings are equal");
    strcpy(s3,s1);
    l1=strlen(s1);
    l2=strlen(s2);
    l3=strlen(s3);
    printf("\ns1=%s\t length=%d characters\n",s1,l1);
    printf("\ns2=%s\t length=%d characters\n",s2,l2);
    printf("\ns3=%s\t length=%d characters\n",s3,l3);
}
```

Program 8.2

Printing Large Block Letters.c —

```
#include <stdio.h>
void blockg(void);   /*Prototype for blockg function */
int main (void)
   {
   printf("\n");
   blockg();
   printf("\n");
   }
/* Print out the Block letter g */
void blockg(void)
   {
   printf("gggggg\n");
   printf("g    g\n");
   printf("g\n");
   printf("g  ggg\n");
   printf("g    g\n");
   printf("gggggg\n");
   }
  It prints out:
gggggg
g    g
g
g  ggg
g    g
gggggg
```

Program 8.3

Computing the factorial of a number.c — It computes repeatedly the factorial of an integer entered by the user. It terminates when the integer entered is not positive.

```
#include <stdio.h>
int fact(int n);
int main(void)
    {
    int current;
    printf("Enter a positive integer [to terminate enter non-positive] > ");
    scanf("%d", &current);
    while (current > 0)
        {
        printf("The factorial of %d is %d\n", current, fact(current));
        printf("Enter a positive integer to terminate enter non-positive>");
        scanf("%d", &current);
        }
    }
/* n is a positive integer. The function returns its factorial */
int fact(int n)
    {
    int lcv;    /* loop control variable */
    int p;      /* set to the product of the first lcv positive integers */
    for(p=1, lcv=2; lcv <= n; p=p*lcv, lcv++);
    return p;
    }
```

Program 8.4

Some simple functions.c Examples of function declarations, definitions, and use

```
#include <stdio.h>
/* Examples of declarations of functions */
void square1(void);  /* Example of a function without input parameters
            and without return value */
void square2(int i);  /* Example of a function with one input parameter
                and without return value */
```

```
int square3(void);   /* Example of a function without input parameters
                      and with integer return value */
int square4(int i);  /* Example of a function with one input parameter
            and with integer return value */
int area(int b, int h); /* Example of a function with two input parameters
             and with integer return value */
/* Main program: Using the various functions */
int main (void)
   {
   square1();    /* Calling the square1 function */
   square2(7);   /* Calling the square2 function using 7 as actual
          parameter corresponding to the formal parameter i */
 printf("The value of square3() is %d\n", square3()); /* Using the square3
                                                function */
 printf("The value of square4(5) is %d\n", square4(5)); /* Using the square4
      function with 5 as actual parameter corresponding to i */
 printf("The value of area(3,7) is %d\n", area(3,7)); /* Using the area
          function with 3, 7 as actual parameters corresponding
      to b, h respectively */
   }

/* Definitions of the functions */
/* Function that reads from standard input an integer and prints
  it out together with its sum */
void square1(void)
   {
  int x;
  printf("Please enter an integer > ");
  scanf("%d", &x);
  printf("The square of %d is %d\n", x, x*x);
   }
/* Function that prints i together with its sum */
void square2(int i)
   {
  printf("The square of %d is %d\n", i, i*i);
   }
/* Function that reads from standard input an integer and returns
  its square */
int square3(void)
   {
```

```
    int x;
  printf("Please enter an integer > ");
  scanf("%d", &x);
  return (x*x);
    }
/* Function that returns the square of i */
int square4(int i)
    {
  return (i*i);
    }

/* Function that returns the area of the rectangle with base b
  and hight h */
int area(int b, int h)
    {
    return (b*h);
    }
The output of this program is:
Please enter an integer > 3
The square of 3 is 9
The square of 7 is 49
Please enter an integer > 4
The value of square3() is 16
The value of square4(5) is 25
The value of area(3,7) is 21
```

Program 8.5

More simple functions.c — More examples of functions

```
#include <stdio.h>
int getint(void); /*It prompts user to enter an integer, which it returns*/
int getmax(int a, int b, int c); /*It returns value of largest of a, b, c*/
/* Main program: Using the various functions */
int main (void)
    {
    int x, y, z;
    x = getint();
    y = getint();
    z = getint();
    printf("The largest of %d, %d, and %d is %d\n", x, y, z, getmax(x,y,z));
```

```
    }
int getint(void)
    {
    int a;
    printf("Please enter an integer > ");
  scanf("%d", &a);
  return(a);
    }
int getmax(int a, int b, int c)
    {
    int m = a;
    if (m<b)
        m = b;
  if (m<c)
        m = c;
  return(m);
    }
```

Program 8.6

Simple example on scope rules.c — Simple example showing effects of the scope rules

```
#include <stdio.h>
int a=0;    /* This is a global variable */
void foo(void);
int main(void)
    {
    int a=2;  /* This is a variable local to main */
    int b=3;  /* This is a variable local to main */
  printf("1. main_b = %d\n", b);
  printf("main_a = %d\n", a);
  foo();
  printf("2. main_b = %d\n", b);
    }
void foo(void)
    {
    int b=4;  /* This is a variable local to foo */
    printf("foo_a = %d\n", a);
    printf("foo_b = %d\n", b);
    }
```

Program 8.7

Another example on scope rules.c — Example on scope rules

```
#include <stdio.h>
int x = 2;
int y = 3;
int z = 4;
void moo(int x, int *y)
    {
    int z;
    x = x+3;
    *y = *y+3;
    z = z+3;  /*Here z is the local z. Notice that it has not been
   initialized. As you see from the output below in this case it was implicitly
   initialized to 0.In general that is not the case and the compiler should give
   you a warning */
    printf("moo :  x = %1d, *y = %1d, y = %1d, z = %1d\n", x,*y,y,z);
    }
int main(void)
    {
    moo(x, &y);
    printf("main: x = %1d1, y = %1d, z = %1d\n", x,y,z);
    }

The output is
moo :  x = 5, *y = 6, y = 1073742056, z = 3
main: x = 21, y = 6, z = 4
```

Program 8.8

string1.c — Simple string operations

String literals.

printf, scanf, %s, %c

strlen

strcpy

strcmp

```
#include <stdio.h>
#define MAXBUFF 128
int main(void)
   {
   char c[] = "012345";
   char line[MAXBUFF];
   int lcv;
   int cmp;
   printf("sizeof(c)= %d\n", sizeof(c));
   printf("sizeof(line)= %d\n", sizeof(line));
   for (lcv=0; lcv<=strlen(c); lcv++)
       printf("c[lcv]= %d = %c\n",c[lcv],c[lcv]);
   printf("Please enter a string : ");
 scanf("%s",line);
 printf("strlen(line) = %d\n", strlen(line));
 printf("line = [%s]\n",line);
 cmp = strcmp(c,line);
 if(cmp<0)
  printf("%s is less than %s\n", c, line);
 else if (c==0)
  printf("%s is equal to %s\n", c, line);
 else
  printf("%s is greater than %s\n", c, line);
 strcpy(line,c);   /*copy the string c into line */
 cmp = strcmp(c,line);
 if(cmp<0)
  printf("%s is less than %s\n", c, line);
 else if (cmp==0)
  printf("%s is equal to %s\n", c, line);
 else
  printf("%s is greater than %s\n", c, line);
   }
```

```
The output of this program:
sizeof(c)= 7
sizeof(line)= 128
c[lcv]= 48 = 0
c[lcv]= 49 = 1
c[lcv]= 50 = 2
c[lcv]= 51 = 3
c[lcv]= 52 = 4
c[lcv]= 53 = 5
c[lcv]= 0 =
Please enter a string : roses are red
strlen(line) = 5
line = [roses]
012345 is less than roses
012345 is equal to 012345
```

Program 8.9

getline.c — Testing a function that reads a line from input.

```
#include <stdio.h>
#define MAXBUF 128
int getline(char line[], int nmax);
int main(void)
    {
    int len;
    char buffer[MAXBUF];
    while(1)
        {
        len = getline(buffer, MAXBUF);
        if (len==0)break;
        printf("len = %d, line = %s\n", len, buffer);
        };
    }
int getline(char line[], int nmax)
    /* It prompts user and reads up to nmax
    * characters into line. It returns number
```

```
* of characters read. ['\n' terminates the line] */
{
int len;
char c;
len = 0;
printf("Enter a string [CR to exit]: ");
while(((c=getchar())!='\n') && len<nmax-1)
    line[len++]=c;
line[len]='\0';
return len;
}
```

Program 8.10

string2.c — Compacting sequences of spaces in a string.
We use two different methods

```
#include <stdio.h>
#define MAXBUFF 128
int getline(char line[], int nmax);
int compact1(char line[]);
int compact2(char line[]);
int main(void)
    {
    char buffer1[MAXBUFF];
    char buffer2[MAXBUFF];
    int len;
    len = getline(buffer1, MAXBUFF);
    printf("You entered : %s\n", buffer1);
    strcpy(buffer2,buffer1);
    printf("Which is : %s\n", buffer2);
    len=compact1(buffer1);
    printf("compact1: len=%d,  %s\n",len, buffer1);
    len=compact2(buffer2);
    printf("compact2: len=%d,  %s\n",len, buffer2);
    }
```

```
int getline(char line[], int nmax)
    /* It prompts user and reads up to nmax
     * characters into line. It returns number
     * of characters read. ['\n' terminates the line] */
    {
    int len;
    char c;
    len = 0;
    printf("Enter a string [CR to exit]: ");
    while(((c=getchar())!='\n') && len<nmax-1)
    line[len++]=c;
    line[len]='\0';
    return len;
    }
int compact1(char line[])
    /* It replaces streaks of spaces in line by a
     * single space. It returns lenght of resulting string.  */
    {
    int cursor=0;      /* Cursor on the line */
    int prevspace = 0; /* True iff preceding position was with a space */
    int lcv=0;         /* Other cursor */
    if(line[cursor]=='\0')
        return 0;
    do{
        if((line[cursor]==' ')&&prevspace)
            {
/*If we have a space preceded by a space, move rest of string left one position */
            for(lcv=cursor;line[lcv];lcv++)
                line[lcv]=line[lcv+1];
            }
        else
            prevspace=(line[cursor++]==' ');
    }while(line[cursor]);
    return cursor;
}
```

```
int compact2(char line[])
/* It replaces streaks of spaces in line by a single space.
 It returns lenght of resulting string.*/
    {
    int cursor=0;      /* Cursor on the line */
    int prevspace = 0; /* True iff preceding position was with a space */
    int lcv = 0;       /* Where we copy characters to */
     do{
       if(!((line[cursor]==' ')&&prevspace)){
       line[lcv++]=line[cursor];
       prevspace=(line[cursor]==' ');
       }
   }while(line[cursor++]);
   return(lcv-1); /*We need the -1 since it counts also the '\0' */
}
```

Program 8.11

number.c - Reading and writing integer as character sequences .Notice that the base for the digits is the constant BASE that I have chosen to be 10. Of course, you use a different value. You might even chose to have the base as a function parameter.

```
#include <stdio.h>
#include <assert.h>
#define BASE 10
/* a is a string. cursor is a position in a such that a[cursor] is a digit.
Return the integer value represented by the longest sequence of digits
in a starting at cursor. On exit cursor will be at the first position
in a that does not contain a digit. Note that we assume that the base for
the number is 10. */
int getNumberToken(char a[], int *cursor)
    {
    int value = 0;
    assert((*cursor) >= 0 && (*cursor) < strlen(a));
     do{
        value = value*BASE + (int)(a[*cursor]) - (int)('0');(*cursor)++;
       }while (isdigit(a[*cursor]));
  return value;
    }
```

```
/* value is a positive integer. a is a character array with n positions.
Store in a as a '\0' terminated string the representation of value as
a string in base BASE. */
void putNumberToken(int value, char a[], int n)
   {
    int k;
    int h, temp;
    assert(value >= 0 && n > 0);
   /* We collect the desired string in reverse order */
    for (k = 0; k < n-1; ++k)
      {
      a[k] = (char)(value%BASE + (int)'0');
      value = value/BASE;
      if (value == 0) break;
      }
   if (k == 0)     /* If value was 0 we still return a '0' */
      a[k] = '0';
   a[++k] = '\0';
  /* Now we put the string in the right order */
   for (h = 0; h < k/2; ++h)
      {
      temp = a[h];
      a[h] = a[k-1-h];
      a[k-1-h] = temp;
      }
   }
void main (void)
   {
   char s[] = "5432";
   int k = 0;
   int val = getNumberToken(s, &k);
   char outs[256];
   printf("val = %d, k = %d\n", val, k);
   putNumberToken(val, outs, 256);
   printf("val = %s\n", outs);
  }
```

Program 8.12

merge.c — Given two sorted sequences of integers, it creates a sorted sequence consisting of all their numbers.

```
#include <stdio.h>
#define NMAX 10
void printIntArray(int a[], int n);
void merge(int c[], int *nc, int a[], int na, int b[], int nb);
int main(void)
  {
  int x[NMAX] = {1,3,5,6,7}; /* The first sorted sequence */
  int y[NMAX] = {2,3,4}; /* The second sorted sequence */
  int z[NMAX+NMAX]; /* The merge sequence */
  int nz;
  merge(z,&nz,x,5,y,3);
  printIntArray(z,nz);
  }
void printIntArray(int a[], int n)
  /* n is the number of elements in the array a.
   * These values are printed out, five per line. */
  {
   int i;
   for (i=0; i<n; )
     {
     printf("\t%d ", a[i++]);
     if (i%5==0)
     printf("\n");
     }
  printf("\n");
  }
void merge(int c[], int *nc, int a[], int na, int b[], int nb){
 /* Given sorted sequences a and b, respectively with na and nb
  * elements, it stores their merge sequence in c and returns
  * the total number of elements in nc */
   int cursora, cursorb, cursorc;
   cursora=cursorb=cursorc=0;
```

```
      while((cursora<na)&&(cursorb<nb))
        if (a[cursora]<=b[cursorb])
            c[cursorc++]=a[cursora++];
        else
            c[cursorc++]=b[cursorb++];
       while(cursora<na)
           c[cursorc++]=a[cursora++];
       while(cursorb<nb)
          c[cursorb++]=b[cursorb++];
      *nc = cursorc;
     }
```

■ ■ ■

9

ARRAYS

OBJECTIVE

In this chapter you will learn about C Programming - Arrays - Declaration of arrays, Initialization of arrays, Multi dimensional Arrays, Elements of multi dimension arrays and Initialization of multidimensional arrays.

9.1 Introduction

• The C language provides a capability of data structure which hold multiple variables of the same data type. Consider the following example

```
int name1 = 101;
int name2 = 232;
int name3 = 231;
```

It becomes increasingly more difficult to keep track of this as the number of variables increase. Arrays offer a solution to this problem. An array is a multi-element box, and uses an indexing system to find each variable stored within it. In C, indexing starts at zero. Arrays, like other variables in C, must be declared before they can be used.

The replacement of the above example using arrays looks like,

```
int names[4];
names[0] = 101;
names[1] = 232;
names[2] = 231;
names[3] = 0;
```

We created an array called *names*, which has space for four integer variables. You may also see that we stored 0 in the last space of the array. This is a common technique used by C programmers to signify the end of an array. Arrays have the following syntax, using square brackets to access each indexed value (called an element). Each element of the set can then be referenced by means of a number called as *index* number or *subscript*.

```
#include <stdio.h>
main()
{
        char word[20];
        word[0] = 'H';
        word[1] = 'e';
        word[2] = 'l';
        word[3] = 'l';
        word[4] = 'o';
        word[5] = 0;
        printf("The contents of word[] is —>%s\n", word );
}
```

Sample Program Output

```
The contents of word[] is Hello
```

9.2 Declaration of Arrays

Like any other variable arrays must be declared before they are used. The general form of declaration is:

```
type variable-name[50];
```

The type specifies the type of the elements that will be contained in the array, such as int float or char and the size indicates the maximum number of elements that can be stored inside the array for ex:

```
float height[50];
```

Declares the height to be an array containing 50 real elements. Any subscripts 0 to 49 are valid. In C the array elements index or subscript begins with number zero. So height [0] refers to the first element of the array. As individual array element can be used anywhere that a normal variable with a statement such as

```
g = grade [50];
```

The statement assigns the value stored in the 50th index of the array to the variable G. More generally if I is declared to be an integer variable, then the statement

```
g=grades [I];
```

Will take the value contained in the element number I of the grades array to assign it to g. so if I were equal to 7 when the above statement is executed, then the value of grades [7] would get assigned to g. A value stored into an element in the array simply by specifying the array element on the left hand side of the equals sign. In the statement

```
grades [100]=95;
```

The value 95 is stored into the element number 100 of the grades array.

The ability to represent a collection of related data items by a single array enables us to develop concise and efficient programs. For example we can very easily sequence through the elements in the array by varying the value of the variable that is used as a subscript into the array. So the for loop

```
for(i=0;i < 100;++i);
sum = sum + grades [i];
```

Will sequence through the first 100 elements of the array grades (elements 0 to 99) and will add the values of each grade into sum. When the for loop is finished, the variable sum will then contain the total of first 100 values of the grades array. In addition to integer constants, integer valued expressions can also be inside the brackets to reference a particular element of the array. So if low and high were defined as integer variables, then the statement

```
next_value=sorted_data[(low+high)/2];
```

would assign to the variable next_value indexed by evaluating the expression (low+high)/2. If low is equal to 1 and high were equal to 9, then the value of sorted_data[5] would be assigned to the next_value and if low were equal to 1 and high were equal to 10 then the value of sorted_data[5] would also be referenced. Just as variables arrays must also be declared before they are used. The declaration of an array involves the type of the element that will be contained in the array such as int, float, char as well as maximum number of elements that will be stored inside the array. The C system needs this latter information in order to determine how much memory space to reserve for the particular array. The declaration int values[10]; would reserve enough space for an array called values that could hold up to 10 integers. Refer to the below given picture to conceptualize the reserved storage space.

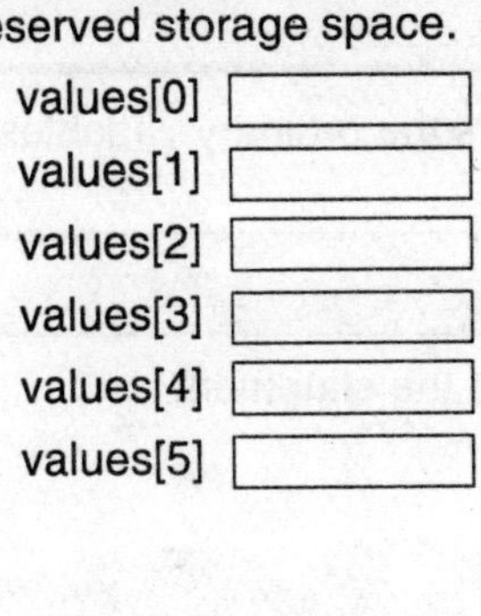

values[6]

values[7]

values[8]

values[9]

The array values stored in the memory.

9.2.1 Some Variations In Declaring Arrays

```
int  numbers[10];
static int numbers[10] = { 34, 27, 16 };
static int numbers[] = { 2, -3, 45, 79, -14, 5, 9, 28, -1, 0 };
static char text[] = "Welcome to New Zealand.";
static float radix[12] = { 134.362, 1913.248 };
double  radians[1000];
```

Program:

```
#include <stdio.h>
main()
{
        int  numbers[100];
        float  averages[20];
        numbers[2] = 10;
        —numbers[2];
        printf("The 3rd element of array numbers is %d\n", numbers[2]);
}
```

Sample Program Output

The 3rd element of array numbers is 9

9.3 Initialization of Arrays

We can initialize the elements in the array in the same way as the ordinary variables when they are declared. The general form of initialization off arrays is:

```
type array_name[size]={list of values};
```

The values in the list care separated by commas, for example the statement

```
int number[3]={0,0,0};
```

Will declare the array size as a array of size 3 and will assign zero to each element if the number of values in the list is less than the number of elements, then only that many elements are initialized. The remaining elements will be set to zero automatically. In the declaration of an array the size may be omitted, in such cases the compiler allocates enough space for all initialized elements. For example the statement

int counter[]={1,2,3};

Will declare the array to contain four elements with initial values 1. this approach works fine as long as we initialize every element in the array. The initialization of arrays in C suffers two drawbacks

(1) There is no convenient way to initialize only selected elements.

(2) There is no shortcut method to initialize large number of elements.

Program:

```
#include <stdio.h>
main()
{
    int x;
    static int  values[] = { 1,2,3,4,5,6,7,8,9 };
    static char  word[] = { 'H','e','l','l','o' };
    for( x = 0; x < 9; ++x )
        printf("Values [%d] is %d\n", x, values[x]);
}

Sample Program Output
Values[0] is 1
Values[1] is 2
....
Values[8] is 9
```

/* Program to count the no. of positive and negative numbers*/

```
#include< stdio.h >
int main( )
{
int a[50],n,count_neg=0,count_pos=0,I;
printf("Enter the size of the array\n");
scanf("%d",&n);
```

```
printf("Enter the elements of the array\n");
for I=0;I < n;I++)
scanf("%d",&a[I]);
for(I=0;I < n;I++)
{
if(a[I] < 0)
count_neg++;
else
count_pos++;
}
printf("There are %d negative numbers in the array\n",count_neg);
printf("There are %d positive numbers in the array\n",count_pos);
}
```

9.4 Multidimensional Arrays

Often there is a need to store and manipulate two dimensional data structure such as matrices & tables. Here the array has two subscripts. One subscript denotes the row & the other the column.

The declaration of two dimension arrays is as follows:

```
data_type array_name[row_size][column_size];
int m[10][20]
```

Here m is declared as a matrix having 10 rows (numbered from 0 to 9) and 20 columns (numbered 0 through 19). The first element of the matrix is m[0][0] and the last row last column is m[9][19]

9.5 Subscripted Variable Rules

Subscripted variables can be double, integer or character. The maximum number of subscripts is dictated by the compiler vendor. Arithmetic expressions may be used for subscripts. Subscripts must be integer valued. A statement must be included in your program which sets aside storage space (dimensions) for your arrays a 2D array in C is treated as a 1D array whose elements are 1D arrays (the rows).

For example,

a 4x3 array of T (where "T" is some data type) may be declared by: "T mat[4][3]", and described by the following scheme:

```
mat == mat[0]   —> I a00 I a01 I a02 I
       mat[1]   —> I a10 I a11 I a12 I
```

mat[2] —> | a20 | a21 | a22 |
mat[3] —> | a30 | a31 | a32 |

The array elements are stored in memory row after row, so the array equation for element "mat[m][n]" of type T is:

address(mat[i][j]) = address(mat[0][0]) + (i * n + j) * size(T)

address(mat[i][j]) = address(mat[0][0]) +
i * n * size(T) +
j * size(T)

address(mat[i][j]) = address(mat[0][0]) +
i * size(row of T) +
j * size(T)

9.6 Elements of Multidimension Arrays

A 2 dimensional array marks [4][3] is shown below figure. The first element is given by marks [0][0] contains 35.5 & second element is marks [0][1] and contains 40.5 and so on.

Marks [0][0] 35.5	Marks [0][1] 40.5	Marks [0][2] 45.5
Marks [1][0] 50.5	Marks [1][1] 55.5	Marks [1][2] 60.5
Marks [2][0]	Marks [2][1]	Marks [2][2]
Marks [3][0]	Marks [3][1]	Marks [3][2]

9.6.1 Initialization of Multidimensional Arrays

Like the one dimension arrays, 2 dimension arrays may be initialized by following their declaration with a list of initial values enclosed in braces

Example:

int table[2][3]={1,2,3,4,5,6};

Initializes the elements of first row first column to 1 and second column to 2. The initialization is done row by row. The above statement can be equivalently written as

int table[2][3]={{1,2,3},{4,5,6}}

By surrounding the elements of each row by braces. C allows arrays of three or more dimensions. The compiler determines the maximum number of dimension. The general form of a multidimensional array declaration is:

```
date_type array_name[s1][s2][s3]…...[sn];
```

Where s is the size of the ith dimension.

float table[5][4][5][3];

/* example program to add two matrices & store the results in the 3rd matrix */

```
#include< stdio.h >
#include< conio.h >
int main()
{
int a[10][10],b[10][10],c[10][10],i,j,m,n,p,q;
clrscr();
printf("enter the order of the matrix\n");
scanf("%d%d",&p,&q);
if(m==p && n==q)
{
printf("matrix can be added\n");
printf("enter the elements of the matrix a");
for(i=0;i < m;i++)
for(j=0;j < n;j++)
scanf("%d",&a[i][j]);
printf("enter the elements of the matrix b");
for(i=0;i < p;i++)
for(j=0;j < q;j++)
scanf("%d",&b[i][j]);
printf("the sum of the matrix a and b is");
for(i=0;i < m;i++)
for(j=0;j < n;j++)
c[i][j]=a[i][j]+b[i][j];
for(i=0;i < m;i++)
{
for(j=0;j < n;j++)
printf("%d\t",&a[i][j]);
printf("\n");
}
}
```

9.7 Static and Dynamic Allocation of Multidimensional Arrays

An array in C is a region of memory in which the elements (chars, ints, etc.) can be accessed using an index (in a 1-dimensional array, e.g. name[0]) or several indices (in a multi-dimensional array, e.g. names[3][0][2]). The first element in a 1-dimensional array x[] is x[0], in a 2-dimensional array x[][] is x[0][0], and so on. In C you can allocate memory for an array using statements such as:

```
char name[32];
int nums[100];
double coords[60][60]
char names[10][20][64];
double space[32][32][32][32];
```

The index of the last element in a 1-dimensional array is one less than the size of the array (e.g. name[31] if the array is declared using char name[32]). In a multidimensional array the indices of the last element are one less than the sizes of each dimension (e.g. names[9][19][63] if the array is declared using char names[10][20][64]). When an array is declared as above, memory is allocated for the elements of the array when the program starts, and this memory remains allocated during the lifetime of the program. This is known as *static* array allocation. It may happen that you don't know how large an array you will need. In this case it is convenient to allocate an array while the program is running. This is known as *dynamic* array allocation. Dynamic allocation of a 1-dimensional array is easily done using the malloc() function. For example, if you wish to allocate an array of 1000 ints then the following code can be used:

```
#include <malloc.h>
#include <stdio.h>
#include <stdlib.h>
int main(void)
{
int *a;
int i=1000;

if ( ( a = (int *)malloc(i*sizeof(int)) ) == NULL )
   {
   printf("\nError, memory not allocated.\n");
   exit(1);
   }

for ( i=0; i<1000; i++ )
   a[i] = i;

// ...

free(a);
}
```

Dynamic allocation of arrays of more than one dimension is not so easily done, because dynamic allocation of an n-dimensional array actually requires dynamic allocation of n 1-dimensional arrays. To allocate a 2-dimensional array you must first allocate memory sufficient to hold all the elements of the array, then allocate memory for pointers to each row of the array. For arrays of more than two dimensions it gets more complicated. To allocate a 3-dimensional array you first allocate memory for the data, then allocate memory for an array of pointers to rows of data within that memory, then allocate memory for an array of pointers to a subset of those pointers. And so on for arrays of higher dimension.

EXERCISE

(1) Declare a character based array called letters of ten elements

Ans:
```
char letters[10];
```

(2) Assign the character value 'Z' to the fourth element of the letters array

Ans:
```
letters[3] = 'Z';
```

(3) Use a for loop to total the contents of an integer array called numbers which has five elements. Store the result in an integer called total.

Ans:
```
for( loop = 0, total = 0; loop < 5; loop++ )
total = total + numbers[loop];
```

(4) Declare a multidimensioned array of floats called balances having three rows and five columns.

Ans:
```
float balances[3][5];
```

(5) Write a for loop to total the contents of the multidimensioned float array balances.

Ans:
```
for( row = 0, total = 0; row < 3; row++ )
for( column = 0; column < 5; column++ )
        total = total + balances[row][column];
```

(6) Assign the text string "Hello" to the character based array words at declaration time.

Ans:
```
static char words[] = "Hello";
```

(7) Assign the text string "Welcome" to the character based array stuff (not at declaration time)

Ans:
```
char stuff[50];
strcpy( stuff, "Welcome" );
```

(8) Use a printf statement to print out the third element of an integer array called totals

> **Ans:** printf("%d\n", totals[2]);

(9) Use a printf statement to print out the contents of the character array called words

> **Ans:** printf("%s\n", words);

(10) Use a scanf statement to read a string of characters into the array words.

> **Ans:** scanf("%s", words);

(11) Write a for loop which will read five characters (use scanf) and deposit them into the character based array words, beginning at element 0.

> **Ans:** for(loop = 0; loop < 5; loop++)
> scanf("%c", &words[loop]);

Program 9.1

Operations on arrays.c — Operations on arrays

```
#include <stdio.h>
int main(void)
    {
    int a[2] = {1,2};  /* The aggregates like {1,2} are literals for arrays */
    int b[2] = {2,3};
    int i;
/* It is legal to use subscripts on arrays, both on the left and on
 * the right hand side of assignments. */
 for(i=0;i<2;i++)
      a[i]=b[i];
/* It is not legal to assign arrays, like in a=b; */
/* The comparison of two distinct arrays with the same content
  * results in FALSE. So below we print "They are not equal"*/
 if(a==b)
      printf("They are equal\n");
 else
      printf("They are not equal\n");
/* The following comparison results in TRUE. */
 if(a==a)
      printf("Of course a is equal to a\n");
```

```
else
        printf("No, a is not equal to a\n");
/* The behavior of comparison is explained when we note that the
 * comparison is a comparison of addresses, not contents.   */
/* We cannot print out an array as a single unit. We have to print out
 * its elements one at a time. */
for(i=0;i<2;i++)
        printf("a[%1d] = %3d\n", i, a[i]);
}
```

Program 9.2

Simple uses of arrays.c — Simple operations with arrays.

```
#include <stdio.h>
#define N 10
void oneWay(void);
void anotherWay(void);
int main(void)
    {
    printf("\noneWay:\n");
    oneWay();
    printf("\nantherWay:\n");
    anotherWay();
    }
/*Array initialized with aggregate */
void oneWay(void)
    {
    int vect[N] = {1,2,3,4,5,6,7,8,9,0};
    int i;
    for (i=0; i<N; i++)
        printf("i = %2d  vect[i] = %2d\n", i, vect[i]);
    }
/*Array initialized with loop */
void anotherWay(void)
    {
```

```
    int vect[N];
  int i;
  for (i=0; i<N; i++)
        vect[i] = i+1;
  for (i=0; i<N; i++)
        printf("i = %2d  vect[i] = %2d\n", i, vect[i]);
  }
```

The output of this program is

One Way:

```
i = 0 vect[i] = 1
i = 1 vect[i] = 2
i = 2 vect[i] = 3
i = 3 vect[i] = 4
i = 4 vect[i] = 5
i = 5 vect[i] = 6
i = 6 vect[i] = 7
i = 7 vect[i] = 8
i = 8 vect[i] = 9
i = 9 vect[i] = 0
```

another Way:

```
i = 0 vect[i] = 1
i = 1 vect[i] = 2
i = 2 vect[i] = 3
i = 3 vect[i] = 4
i = 4 vect[i] = 5
i = 5 vect[i] = 6
i = 6 vect[i] = 7
i = 7 vect[i] = 8
i = 8 vect[i] = 9
i = 9 vect[i] = 10
```

Program 9.3

Reading, writing, reversing an integer array.c — Read/writing/reversing integer arrays

```
#include <stdio.h>
#define NMAX 10
void intSwap(int *x, int *y);
int getIntArray(int a[], int nmax, int sentinel);
void printIntArray(int a[], int n);
void reverseIntArray(int a[], int n);
int main(void)
    {
    int x[NMAX];
    int hmny;
    hmny = getIntArray(x, NMAX, 0);
    printf("The array was: \n");
    printIntArray(x,hmny);
    reverseIntArray(x,hmny);
    printf("after reverse it is:\n");
    printIntArray(x,hmny);
    }
void intSwap(int *x, int *y)
    /* It swaps the content of x and y */
    {
    int temp = *x;
    *x = *y;
    *y = temp;
    }
void printIntArray(int a[], int n)
  /* n is the number of elements in the array a.
   * These values are printed out, five per line. */
    {
    int i;
    for (i=0; i<n; )
        {
        printf("\t%d ", a[i++]);
        if (i%5==0)
```

```
            printf("\n");
        }
    printf("\n");
    }
int getIntArray(int a[], int nmax, int sentinel)
    /* It reads up to nmax integers and stores then in a; sentinel
     * terminates input. */
    {
    int n = 0;
    int temp;
        do {
        printf("Enter integer [%d to terminate] : ", sentinel);
        scanf("%d", &temp);
        if (temp==sentinel) break;
        if (n==nmax)
            printf("array is full\n");
        else
            a[n++] = temp;
        }while (1);
    return n;
    }
void reverseIntArray(int a[], int n)
    /* It reverse the order of the first n elements of a */
    {
    int i;
    for(i=0;i<n/2;i++)
        {
        intSwap(&a[i],&a[n-i-1]);
        }
}
```

Program 9.4

linear.c — Read an integer array and then do linear searches.

```
#include <stdio.h>
#define NMAX 10
int getIntArray(int a[], int nmax, int sentinel);
void printIntArray(int a[], int n);
int linear(int a[], int n, int who);
int main(void)
  {
  int x[NMAX];
  int hmny;
  int who;
  int where;
  hmny = getIntArray(x, NMAX, 0);
  printf("The array was: \n");
  printIntArray(x,hmny);
  printf("Now we do linear searches on this data\n");
 do
  {
  printf("Enter integer to search for [0 to terminate] : ");
  scanf("%d", &who);
  if(who==0)break;
  where = linear(x,hmny,who);
  if (where<0)
     {
     printf("Sorry, %d is not in the array\n",who);
     }
  else
     printf("%d is at position %d\n",who,where);
 }while(1);
  }
void printIntArray(int a[], int n)
  /* n is the number of elements in the array a.
   * These values are printed out, five per line. */
  {
```

```
int i;
for (i=0; i<n; )
    {
    printf("\t%d ", a[i++]);
    if (i%5==0)
        printf("\n");
    }
printf("\n");
}
int getIntArray(int a[], int nmax, int sentinel)
/* It reads up to nmax integers and stores then in a; sentinel
 * terminates input. */
{
int n = 0;
int temp;
do {
printf("Enter integer [%d to terminate] : ", sentinel);
scanf("%d", &temp);
if (temp==sentinel) break;
if (n==nmax)
printf("array is full\n");
else
    a[n++] = temp;
}while (1);
return n;
}
int linear(int a[], int n, int who)
/* Given the array a with n elements, searches for who.
 * It returns its position if found, otherwise it returns
 * -1.   */
{
int lcv;
for (lcv=0;lcv<n;lcv++)
if(who == a[lcv])return lcv;
return (-1);
}
```

Program 9.5

```
shift.c — It reads a sequence of positive integers. It stores it
 *        in an array, then it prompts the user to enter an
 *        integer, and then rotates clockwise the content of the
 *        array a corresponding number of positions. The contents
 *        the array are printed out whenever it changes.
 *        For example, if the sequence was
 *            1,2,3,4,5
 *        and the number 3 is entered, the array becomes
 *            3,4,5,1,2
 *        and if th' number 11 is now entered, the array becomes
 *            2,3,4,5,1
 *        and if the number -4 is now entered, the array becomes
 *            1,2,3,4,5 */
```

```
#include <stdio.h>
#define MAXN 8
/* It prints the current content on the array a with n elements */
void printarray(int a[], int n);
/* I will assume first that I have a number of functions then I will
 * write them. */
/* Given an array a with n values, shift rotates
 * its content m positions, clockwise. */
void shift(int a[], int n, int m);
/* getint prompts the user to enter a positive integer and returns
 * its value. */
int getint(void);
/* It requests the user to enter positive integers and stores
 * them in a. It returns in n the number of integers stored
 * in the array. */
void getarray(int a[], int *n);
int main(void)
  {
  int table[MAXN]; /* array where we store the sequence */
  int howmany=0;   /* number of elements in sequence */
```

```
int amount;   /* amount of shift */
getarray(table, &howmany);
if (howmany==0)
    {
    printf("Sorry, you entered the null sequence. Good bye.\n");
    }
Else
    {
    do {
    printarray(table,howmany);
    printf("By how much do you want to shift[0 to terminate]? ");
    scanf("%d",&amount);
    if (amount!=0)
        shift(table,howmany,amount);
    }while(amount!=0);
    }
}

/* Given an array a with n values, shift rotates
 * its content m positions, clockwise. */
void shift(int a[], int n, int m)
  {
  int temp[MAXN];
  int lcv;
  if (m<0)
  m = n-(abs(m)%n);
  for (lcv=0;lcv<n;lcv++)
      temp[(lcv+m)%n] = a[lcv];
  for (lcv=0; lcv<n;lcv++)
      a[lcv]=temp[lcv];
  }
/* getint prompts the user to enter a positive integer and returns
* its value.  */
int getint(void)
  {
  int answer;
```

```
        printf("Please enter a positive integer [<=0 to terminate] : ");
        scanf("%d", &answer);
        return answer;
        }
/* It requests the user to enter positive integers and stores
 * them in a. It returns in n the number of integers stored
 * in the array. */
 void getarray(int a[], int *n)
        {
        int answer;
        int i=0;
            do {
            answer = getint();
            if (answer>0 && (i<MAXN))
            a[i++]=answer;
            }while(answer>0 && (i<MAXN));
       *n = i;
        }
/* It prints the current content of the array a with n eler..ents */
        void printarray(int a[], int n)
        {
        int lcv;
        for (lcv=0;lcv<n;lcv++)
            {
            printf("   %d",a[lcv]);
            }
        printf("\n");
        }
```

Program 9.6

binary.c - Binary search using two methods. The first is more intuitive, but it is slower.

```
#include <stdio.h>
#include <sys/time.h>
/* Given a sorted array with n elements, we search for who using binary search.
We return a position where found, or -1 if not there */
int binary1(int n, int a[n], int who)
   {
   int left = 0;
   int right = n-1;
   while (left <= right)
      {
      int mid = (left + right) /2;
      if (who < a[mid])
         right = mid - 1;
      else if (who > a[mid])
         left = mid + 1;
      else
         return mid;
      }
   return -1;
   }
/*Given a sorted array with n elements, we search for who using binary search.
We return a position where found, or -1 if not there */
int binary2(int n, int a[n], int who)
   {
   int p = n/2;
   while (n > 0)
      {
      n = n/2;
      if (who < a[p])
         {
         p -= n;
         }
      else if (who > a[p])
```

```
            {
            p += n;
            }
          else
            return p;
            }
        return -1;
        }
    /* Returns the difference in microseconds between before and after */
    long timediff(struct timeval before, struct timeval after)
        {
        long sec = after.tv_sec - before.tv_sec;
        long microsec = after.tv_usec - before.tv_usec;
        return 1000000*sec + microsec;
        }
    int main()
        {
        int a[] = {1,3,5,7,9,11,13,15,17,19,21,23,25,27,29,31,33};
        int n = sizeof(a)/sizeof(int);
        int where;
        struct timeval before;
        struct timeval after;
        int k;
        int j;
        gettimeofday(&before, NULL);
        for (j = 0; j < 1000000; j++)
        for (k = 0; k < 2*n+1; k++)
            {
            where = binary1(n, a, k);
            printf("who = %d, \tvalue = %d\n", k, where);
            }
        gettimeofday(&after, NULL);
        printf("before=[%ld,%ld], after=[%ld,%ld]\n",
            before.tv_sec,before.tv_usec,after.tv_sec, after.tv_usec);
        printf("The difference is %ld\n", timediff(before, after));
```

```
printf("—————————————————————————————\n");
gettimeofday(&before, NULL);
for (j = 0; j < 1000000; j++)
for (k = 0; k < 2*n+1; k++)
    {
    where = binary2(n, a, k);
    printf("who = %d, \tvalue = %d\n", k, where);
    }
gettimeofday(&after, NULL);
printf("before=[%ld,%ld], after=[%ld,%ld]\n", before.tv_sec,
    before.tv_usec,after.tv_sec, after.tv_usec);
printf("The difference is %ld\n", timediff(before, after));
return 0;
}
```

Program 9.7

selection.c — Read an integer array, print it, then sort it and
* print it. Use the selection sort method.

```
#include <stdio.h>
#define NMAX 10
int getIntArray(int a[], int nmax, int sentinel);
void printIntArray(int a[], int n);
void selectionSort(int a[], int n);
int main(void)
    {
    int x[NMAX];
    int hmny;
    int who;
    int where;
    hmny = getIntArray(x, NMAX, 0);
    if (hmny==0)
        printf("This is the empty array!\n");
    else
        {
```

```
        printf("The array was: \n");
        printIntArray(x,hmny);
        selectionSort(x,hmny);
        printf("The sorted array is: \n");
        printIntArray(x,hmny);
        }
    }
void printIntArray(int a[], int n)
    /* n is the number of elements in the array a.
     * These values are printed out, five per line. */
    {
    int i;
    for (i=0; i<n; )
        {
        printf("\t%d ", a[i++]);
        if (i%5==0)
            printf("\n");
        }
    printf("\n");
    }
int getIntArray(int a[], int nmax, int sentinel)
    /* It reads up to nmax integers and stores then in a; sentinel
     * terminates input. */
    {
    int n = 0;
    int temp;
        do {
        printf("Enter integer [%d to terminate] : ", sentinel);
        scanf("%d", &temp);
        if (temp==sentinel) break;
        if (n==nmax)
            printf("array is full\n");
        else
            a[n++] = temp;
        }while (1);
    return n;
```

```
}
void selectionSort(int a[], int n)
/* It sorts in non-decreasing order the first N positions of A. It uses
 * the selection sort method. */
   {
   int lcv;
   int rh;        /*Elements in interval rh..n-1 are in their final position*/
   int where;   /*Position where we have current maximum*/
   int temp;    /*Used for swapping*/
   for(rh=n-1;rh>0;rh—)
      {
  /*Find position of largest element in range 0..rh*/
      where = 0;
      for (lcv=1;lcv<=rh;lcv++)
         if (a[lcv]>a[where])
            where = lcv;
         temp = a[where];
         a[where] = a[rh];
         a[rh] = temp;
      }
   }
```

Program 9.8

bubble.c — Read an integer array, print it, then sort it and
* print it. Use the bubble sort method. */

```
#include <stdio.h>
#define NMAX 10
int getIntArray(int a[], int nmax, int sentinel);
void printIntArray(int a[], int n);
void bubbleSort(int a[], int n);
int main(void)
   {
   int x[NMAX];
   int hmny;
```

```
        int who;
        int where;
        hmny = getIntArray(x, NMAX, 0);
        if (hmny==0)
            printf("This is the empty array!\n");
        else
            {
            printf("The array was: \n");
            printIntArray(x,hmny);
            bubbleSort(x,hmny);
            printf("The sorted array is: \n");
            printIntArray(x,hmny);
            }
        }
    void printIntArray(int a[], int n)
        /* n is the number of elements in the array a.
         * These values are printed out, five per line. */
        {
        int i;
        for (i=0; i<n; )
            {
            printf("\t%d ", a[i++]);
            if (i%5==0)
            printf("\n");
            }
        printf("\n");
        }
    int getIntArray(int a[], int nmax, int sentinel)
        /* It reads up to nmax integers and stores then in a; sentinel
         * terminates input. */
        {
        int n = 0;
        int temp;
            do {
            printf("Enter integer [%d to terminate] : ", sentinel);
            scanf("%d", &temp);
```

```
        if (temp==sentinel) break;
        if (n==nmax)
            printf("array is full\n");
        else
            a[n++] = temp;
        }while (1);
    return n;
    }
void bubbleSort(int a[], int n)
/* It sorts in non-decreasing order the first N positions of A. It uses
 * the bubble sort method. */
    {
    int lcv;
    int limit = n-1;
    int temp;
    int lastChange;
  while (limit)
        {
        lastChange = 0;
        for (lcv=0;lcv<limit;lcv++)
    /* Notice that the values in positions LIMIT+1 .. N are in
     * their final position, i.e. they are sorted right */
            if (a[lcv]>a[lcv+1])
                {
                temp = a[lcv];
                a[lcv] = a[lcv+1];
                a[lcv+1] = temp;
                lastChange = lcv;
                }
            limit = lastChange;
        }
    }
```

Program 9.9

program for List Implementation

```
#include<stdio.h>
#include<conio.h>
int main()
{
void read(int *,int);
void dis(int *,int);
int a[5],i,sum=0;
clrscr();
printf("Enter the elements of list \n");
read(a,5);      /*read the list*/
printf("The list elements are  \n");
dis(a,5);
for(i=0;i<5;i++)
    {
        sum+=a[i];

printf("The sum of the elements of the list  is %d\n",sum);
getch();
}
void read(int c[],int i)
{
int j;
for(j=0;j<i;j++)
        scanf("%d",&c[j]);
fflush(stdin);
}
void dis(int d[],int i)
{
int j;
for(j=0;j<i;j++)
    printf("%d  ",d[j]);
    printf("\n");
}
```

Program 9.10

program to Add Element to the List

```
#include<stdio.h>
#include<conio.h>
int main()
{
void read(int *,int);
void dis(int *,int);
int a[5],i,sum=0;
    clrscr();
printf("Enter the elements of array \n");
read(a,5);      /*read the array*/
printf("The array elements are  \n");
dis(a,5);
}
 void read(int c[],int i)
{
int j;
for(j=0;j<i;j++)
    scanf("%d",&c[j]);
  fflush(stdin);
 }

  void dis(int d[],int i)
{
int j;
for(j=0;j<i;j++)
        printf("%d  ",d[j]);
    printf("\n");
}
```

Program 9.11

program to Add Element Between List

```
#include<stdio.h>
#include<conio.h>
int main()
{
void read(int *,int);
void dis(int *,int);
void add(int * ,int *,int * ,int);
int a[5],b[5],c[5],i;
    clrscr();
printf("Enter the elements of first list \n");
read(a,5);      /*read the  first list*/
printf("The elements of first list are  \n");
dis(a,5);  /*Display the first  list*/
printf("Enter the elements of second list \n");
read(b,5);      /*read the second list*/
printf("The  elements of second list are  \n");
dis(b,5);   /*Display the second  list*/
add(a,b,c,l);
printf("The resultant list  is \n");
dis(c,5);
getch();
}
void add(int a[],int b[],ibt c[],int l)
{
for(i=0;i<5;i++)
    {
        c[i]=a[i]+b[i];
        }
}
void read(int c[],int i)
{
int j;
for(j=0;j<i;j++)
```

```
        scanf("%d",&c[j]);
fflush(stdin);
}
void dis(int d[],int i)
{
int j;
        for(j=0;j<i;j++)
    printf("%d  ",d[j]);
    printf("\n");
}
```

Program 9.12

program to Inverse List

```
#include<stdio.h>
#include<conio.h>
int main()
{
void read(int *,int);
void   dis(int *,int);
void  inverse(int *,int);
int a[5],i;
clrscr();
read(a,5);
dis(a,5);
inverse(a,5);
dis(a,5);
getch();
}
void read(int c[],int i)
{
int j;
printf("Enter the list \n");
for(j=0;j<i;j++)
        scanf("%d",&c[j]);
```

```
fflush(stdin);
}
void dis(int d[],int i)
{
int j;
printf("The list is \n");
for(j=0;j<i;j++)
        printf("%d  ",d[j]);
    printf("\n");
}
void inverse(int inver_a[],int j)
{
int i,temp;
j—;
for(i=0;i<(j/2);i++)
    {
    temp=inver_a[i];
        inver_a[i]=inver_a[j];
        inver_a[j]=temp;
        j—;
        }
}
```

Program 9.13

program to Merger List

```
#include<stdio.h>
#include<conio.h>
int main()
{
void read(int *,int);
void dis(int *,int);
void sort(int *,int);
void merge(int *,int *,int *,int);
int a[5],b[5],c[10];
clrscr();
```

```
printf("Enter the elements of first list \n");
read(a,5);      /*read the list*/
printf("The elements of first list are  \n");
dis(a,5);  /*Display the first list*/
printf("Enter the elements of second list \n");
read(b,5);      /*read the list*/
printf("The elements of second list are  \n");
dis(b,5);  /*Display the second list*/
sort(a,5);
printf("The sorted list a is:\n");
dis(a,5);
sort(b,5);
   printf("The sorted list b is:\n");
dis(b,5);
   merge(a,b,c,5);
printf("The elements of merged list is  \n");
dis(c,10);  /*Display the merged list*/
getch();
}
void read(int c[],int i)
{
int j;
for(j=0;j<i;j++)
        scanf("%d",&c[j]);
fflush(stdin);
}
void dis(int d[],int i)
{
int j;
for(j=0;j<i;j++)
        printf("%d  ",d[j]);
printf("\n");
}
void sort(int arr[] ,int k)
{
int temp;
int i,j;
for(i=0;i<k;i++)
   {
```

```
        for(j=0;j<k-i-1;j++)
            {
            if(arr[j]<arr[j+1])
                {
                temp=arr[j];
                arr[j]=arr[j+1];
                arr[j+1]=temp;
                }
            }
        }
}
void merge(int a[],int b[],int c[],int k)
{
    int ptra=0,ptrb=0,ptrc=0;
    while(ptra<k && ptrb<k)
        {
        if(a[ptra] < b[ptrb])
            {
            c[ptrc]=b[ptrb];
            ptrb++;
            }
        else
            {
            c[ptrc]=a[ptra];
            ptra++;
            }
        ptrc++;
        }
while(ptra<k)
        {
        c[ptrc]=a[ptra];
        ptra++;ptrc++;
        }
while(ptrb<k)
        {
        c[ptrc]=b[ptrb];
        ptrb++;  ptrc++;
        }
}
```

Program 9.14

program to find transpose matrix

```
#include<stdio.h>
#include<conio.h>
#define ROW 3
#define COL 3
int main()
{
void read(int a[][COL],int,int);
void dis(int a[][COL],int,int);
void trans(int a[][COL],int b[][COL],int,int);
int a[3][3],b[3][3],i,j;
clrscr();
read(a,ROW,COL);
printf("\nThe matrix is \n");
dis(a,ROW,COL);
trans(a,b,ROW,COL);
printf("The Tranpose of the matrix is\n");
dis(b,ROW,COL);
getch();
}
void read(int c[3][3] ,int i ,int k)
{
int j,l;
printf("Enter the array \n");
for(j=0;j<i;j++)
        for(l=0;l<k;l++)
              scanf("%d",&c[j][l]);
fflush(stdin);
}
void dis(int d[3][3 ],int i,int k)
{
int j,l;
for(j=0;j<i;j++)
     {
```

```
            for(l=0;l<k;l++)
                printf("%d  ",d[j][l]);
            printf("\n");
            }
    }
    void trans(int mat[][3],int tr_mat[][3], int k ,int l)
    {
    int i,j;
        for(i=0;i<k;i++)
            for(j=0;j<l;j++)
                {
                tr_mat[i][j]=mat[j][i];
                }
    }
```

Program 9.15

program for saddle point

```
#include<stdio.h>
#include<conio.h>
#define ROW 3
#define COL 3
int main()
{
void read(int a[][COL],int,int);
void dis(int a[][COL],int,int);
int sadd_pt(int a[][COL],int,int,int *,int*);
int i,a[3][3],m=0,n=0;
clrscr();
read(a,ROW,COL);
printf("\nThe matrix is \n");
dis(a,ROW,COL);
i=sadd_pt(a,3,3,&m,&n);
printf("The Saddle Point is %d &its poistion is row : %d col :
%d\n",i,m+1,n+1);
```

```
getch();
}
void read(int c[][3] ,int i ,int k)
{
int j,l;
printf("Enter the array \n");
for(j=0;j<i;j++)
        for(l=0;l<k;l++)
            scanf("%d",&c[j][l]);
fflush(stdin);
}
void dis(int d[][3],int i,int k)
{
int j,l;
for(j=0;j<i;j++)
    {
        for(l=0;l<k;l++)
            printf("\t%d",d[j][l]);
        printf("\n");
        }
}
int sadd_pt(int mat[][3],int k ,int l,int *row,int *col)
{
    int min=32767,i=0,j,m,n,p=0;
    while(i<k)
        {
        min=32767;
        m=i;
        p=0;
        for(j=0;j<l;j++)
            {
            if(mat[i][j]<min)
                {
                min=mat[i][j];
                n=j;
                }
```

```
            }
        for(j=0;j<k;j++)
            if(min>=mat[j][n])
        p++;
        if(p==3)
            {
            *row=m;
            *col=n;
            return(min);
            }
        i++;
        }
printf("No Saddle Point exists\n");
    getch();
    exit(0);
    }
```

Program 9.16

program for Linear Search

```
#include <stdio.h>
#define MAX 10
void lsearch(int list[],int n,int element)
{
int i, flag = 0;
for(i=0;i<n;i++)
        if( list[i] == element)
            {
            printf(" The element whose value is %d is present at
                        position %d in list\n",element,i);
            flag =1;
        break;
        }
if( flag == 0)
    printf("The element whose value is %d is not present in the
```

```
        list\n",element);
}
void readlist(int list[],int n)
{
int i;
printf("Enter the elements\n");
for(i=0;i<n;i++)
    scanf("%d",&list[i]);
}
void printlist(int list[],int n)
{
int i;
printf("The elements of the list are: \n");
for(i=0;i<n;i++)
    printf("%d\t",list[i]);
}
int main()
{
int list[MAX], n, element;
printf("Enter the number of elements in the list max = 10\n");
scanf("%d",&n);
readlist(list,n);
printf("\nThe list before sorting is:\n");
printlist(list,n);
printf("\nEnter the element to be searched\n");
scanf("%d",&element);
lsearch(list,n,element);
}
```

■ ■ ■

Part – III

10. Pointers
11. Structures and Unions
12. File Management

10

POINTERS

OBJECTIVE

In this chapter you will learn about C Programming - Pointers, Pointer declaration, Address operator, Pointer expressions & Pointer arithmetic operations, Pointers and function, Call by value, Call by reference, Pointer to arrays, Pointers and structures, Pointers on pointer. Dynamic Memory Allocation. Memory allocations process, allocating a block of memory, Allocating multiple blocks of memory, releasing the used space and to alter the size of allocated memory.

10.1 Introduction

If you want to be proficient in the writing of code in the C programming language, you must have a thorough working knowledge of how to use pointers. Unfortunately, C pointers appear to represent a stumbling block to newcomers, particularly those coming from other computer languages such as Fortran, Pascal or Basic. To aid those newcomers in the understanding of pointers I have written the following material. To get the maximum benefit from this material, I feel it is important that the user be able to run the code in the various listings contained in the article. I have attempted, therefore, to keep all code ANSI compliant so that it will work with any ANSI compliant compiler. I have also tried to carefully block the code within the text. That way, with the help of an ASCII text editor, you can copy a given block of code to a new file and compile it on your system. I recommend that readers do this as it will help in understanding the material

In C a pointer is a variable that points to or references a memory location in which data is stored. Each memory cell in the computer has an address that can be used to access that location so a pointer variable points to a memory location we can access and change the contents of this memory location via the pointer.

10.2 What is a pointer?

One of those things beginners in C find difficult is the concept of pointers. The purpose of this tutorial is to provide an introduction to pointers and their use to these beginners. I have found that often the main reason beginners have a problem with pointers is that they have a weak or minimal feeling for variables, (as they are used in C). Thus we start with a discussion of C variables in general.

Pointer declaration:

A pointer is a variable that contains the memory location of another variable. The syntax is as shown below. You start by specifying the type of data stored in the location identified by the pointer. The asterisk tells the compiler that you are creating a pointer variable. Finally you give the name of the variable.

```
type * variable name
```

Example:

```
int *ptr;
float *string;
```

10.2.1 Address operator

Once we declare a pointer variable we must point it to something we can do this by assigning to the pointer the address of the variable you want to point as in the following example:

```
ptr=&num;
```

This places the address where num is stores into the variable ptr. If num is stored in memory 21260 address then the variable ptr has the value 21260.

/* A program to illustrate pointer declaration*/

```
main()
{
int  *ptr;
int sum;
sum=45;
ptr=•
printf ("\n Sum is %d\n", sum);
printf ("\n The sum pointer is %d", ptr);
}
```

We will get the same result by assigning the address of num to a regular(non pointer) variable. The benefit is that we can also refer to the pointer variable as *ptr the asterisk tells to the computer that we are not interested in the value 21260 but in the value stored in that memory location. While the value of pointer is 21260 the value of sum is 45 however we can assign a value to the pointer *ptr as in *ptr=45. This means place the value 45 in the memory address pointer by the variable ptr. Since the pointer contains the address 21260 the value 45 is placed in that memory location. And since this is the location of the variable num the value also becomes 45. this shows how we can change the value of pointer directly using a pointer and the indirection pointer.

Program to display the contents of the variable their address using pointer variable

```
include< stdio.h >
{
int num, *intptr;
float x, *floptr;
char ch, *cptr;
num=123;
x=12.34;
ch='a';
intptr=&x;
cptr=&ch;
floptr=&x;
printf("Num %d stored at address %u\n",*intptr,intptr);
printf("Value %f stored at address %u\n",*floptr,floptr);
printf("Character %c stored at address %u\n",*cptr,cptr);
}
```

10.3 Pointer Expressions and Pointer Arithmetic

Like other variables pointer variables can be used in expressions. For example if p1 and p2 are properly declared and initialized pointers, then the following statements are valid.

```
y=*p1**p2;
sum=sum+*p1;
z= 5* - *p2/p1;
*p2= *p2 + 10;
```

C allows us to add integers to or subtract integers from pointers as well as to subtract one pointer from the other. We can also use short hand operators with the pointers p1+=; sum+=*p2; etc., we can also compare pointers by using relational operators the expressions such as p1 >p2 , p1==p2 and p1!=p2 are allowed.

Program to illustrate the pointer expression and pointer arithmetic

```
#include< stdio.h >
main()
{
int ptr1,ptr2;
int a,b,x,y,z;
a=30;b=6;
ptr1=&a;
ptr2=&b;
x=*ptr1+ *ptr2 –6;
y=6*- *ptr1/ *ptr2 +30;
printf("\nAddress of a +%u",ptr1);
printf("\nAddress of b %u",ptr2);
printf("\na=%d, b=%d",a,b);
printf("\nx=%d,y=%d",x,y);
ptr1=ptr1 + 70;
ptr2= ptr2;
printf("\na=%d, b=%d",a,b);
}
```

10.4 Pointers and Function

The pointer are very much used in a function declaration. Sometimes only with a pointer a complex function can be easily represented and success. The usage of the pointers in a function definition may be classified into two groups.

1. Call by reference
2. Call by value.

Call by value:

We have seen that a function is invoked there will be a link established between the formal and actual parameters. A temporary storage is created where the value of actual parameters is stored. The formal parameters picks up its value from storage area the mechanism of data transfer between actual and formal parameters allows the actual parameters mechanism of data transfer is referred as call by value. The corresponding formal parameter represents a local variable in the called function. The current value of corresponding actual parameter becomes the initial value of formal parameter. The value of formal parameter may be changed in the body of the actual parameter. The value of formal parameter may be changed in the body of the subprogram by assignment or input statements. This will not change the value of actual parameters.

```
#Include< stdio.h >
int main()
{
int x,y;
x=20;
y=30;
printf("\n Value of a and b before function call =%d %d",a,b);
fncn(x,y);
printf("\n Value of a and b after function call =%d %d",a,b);
}

fncn(p,q)
int p,q;
{
p=p+p;
q=q+q;
}
```

Call by Reference:

When we pass address to a function the parameters receiving the address should be pointers. The process of calling a function by using pointers to pass the address of the variable is known as call by reference. The function which is called by reference can change the values of the variable used in the call.

Example of call by reference

```
Include< stdio.h >
int main()
{
int x,y;
x=20;
y=30;
printf("\n Value of a and b before function call =%d %d",a,b);
fncn(&x,&y);
printf("\n Value of a and b after function call =%d %d",a,b);
}
fncn(p,q)
int p,q;
{
*p=*p+*p;
*q=*q+*q;
}
```

10.5 Pointer to Arrays

An array is actually very much like pointer. We can declare the arrays first element as a[0] or as int *a because a[0] is an address and *a is also an address the form of declaration is equivalent. The difference is pointer is a variable and can appear on the left of the assignment operator that is lvalue. The array name is constant and cannot appear as the left side of assignment operator.

A program to display the contents of array using pointer

```
#include<stdio.h>
main()
{
int a[100];
int i,j,n;
printf("\nEnter the elements of the array\n");
```

```
scanf("%d",&n);
printf("Enter the array elements");
for(I=0;I< n;I++)
scanf("%d",&a[I]);
printf("Array element are");
for(ptr=a,ptr< (a+n);ptr++)
printf("Value of a[%d]=%d stored at address %u",j+=,*ptr,ptr);
}
```

Strings are characters arrays and here last element is \0 arrays and pointers to char arrays can be used to perform a number of string functions.

10.6 Pointers and Structures: *(Read Chapter Structure and Union)*

We know the name of an array stands for the address of its zero'th element the same concept applies for names of arrays of structures. Suppose item is an array variable of struct type. Consider the following declaration:

```
struct products
{
char name[30];
int manufac;
float net;
item[2],*ptr;
}
```

this statement declares item as array of two elements, each type struct products and ptr as a pointer data objects of type struct products, the assignment ptr=item; would assign the address of zeroth element to product[0]. Its members can be accessed by using the following notation.

```
ptr- >name;
ptr- >manufac;
ptr- >net;
```

The symbol - > is called arrow pointer and is made up of minus sign and greater than sign. Note that ptr- > is simple another way of writing product[0]. When the pointer is incremented by one it is made to pint to next record ie item[1]. The following statement will print the values of members of all the elements of the product array.

```
for(ptr=item; ptr< item+2;ptr++)
printf("%s%d%f\n",ptr- >name,ptr- >manufac,ptr- >net);
```

We could also use the notation

```
(*ptr).number
```

to access the member number. The parenthesis around ptr are necessary because the member operator '.' Has a higher precedence than the operator*.

10.7 Pointers on Pointer

While pointers provide enormous power and flexibility to the programmers, they may use cause manufactures if not properly handled. Consider the following precautions using pointers to prevent errors. We should make sure that we know where each pointer is pointing in a program. Here are some general observations and common errors that might be useful to remember. A pointer contains garbage until it is initialized. Since compilers cannot detect uninitialized or wrongly initialized pointers, the errors may not be known until we execute the program remember that even if we are able to locate a wrong result, it may not provide any evidence for us to suspect problems in the pointers. The abundance of c operators is another cause of confusion that leads to errors. For example the expressions such as

```
*ptr++, *p[],(ptr).member
```

etc. should be carefully used. A proper understanding of the precedence and associativity rules should be carefully used.

10.8 Dynamic Memory Allocation

In programming we may come across situations where we may have to deal with data, which is dynamic in nature. The number of data items may change during the execution of a program. The number of customers in a queue can increase or decrease during the process at any time. When the list grows we need to allocate more memory space to accommodate additional data items. Such situations can be handled more easily by using dynamic techniques. Dynamic data items at run time, thus optimizing file usage of storage space.

The process of allocating memory at run time is known as dynamic memory allocation. Although C does not inherently have this facility there are four library routines which allow this function.

Many languages permit a programmer to specify an array size at run time. Such languages have the ability to calculate and assign during executions, the memory space required by the variables in the program. But C inherently does not have this facility but supports with memory management functions, which can be used to allocate and free memory during the program execution. The following functions are used in C for purpose of memory management.

Function	Task
Malloc	Allocates memory requests size of bytes and returns a pointer to the Ist byte of allocated space
Calloc	Allocates space for an array of elements initializes them to zero and returns a pointer to the memory
Free	Frees previously allocated space
Realloc	Modifies the size of previously allocated space.

10.9 Memory Allocations Process

According to the conceptual view the program instructions and global and static variable in a permanent storage area and local area variables are stored in stacks. The memory space that is located between these two regions in available for dynamic allocation during the execution of the program. The free memory region is called the heap. The size of heap keeps changing when program is executed due to creation and death of variables that are local for functions and blocks. Therefore it is possible to encounter memory overflow during dynamic allocation process. In such situations, the memory allocation functions mentioned above will return a null pointer.

10.9.1 Allocating a block of memory

A block mf memory may be allocated using the function malloc. The malloc function reserves a block of memory of specified size and returns a pointer of type void. This means that we can assign it to any type of pointer. It takes the following form:

```
ptr= (cast-type*) malloc (byte-size);
```

ptr is a pointer of type cast-type the malloc returns a pointer (of cast type) to an area of memory with size byte-size.

Example:

```
x= (int*) malloc (100*sizeof (int));
```

On successful execution of this statement a memory equivalent to 100 times the area of int bytes is reserved and the address of the first byte of memory allocated is assigned to the pointer x of type int

10.9.2 Allocating multiple blocks of memory

Calloc is another memory allocation function that is normally used to request multiple blocks of storage each of the same size and then sets all bytes to zero.

The general form of calloc is:

```
ptr=(cast-type*) calloc(n, elem-size);
```

The above statement allocates contiguous space for n blocks each size of elements size bytes. All bytes are initialized to zero and a pointer to the first byte of the allocated region is returned. If there is not enough space a null pointer is returned.

10.10 Releasing the Used Space

Compile time storage of a variable is allocated and released by the system in accordance with its storage class. With the dynamic runtime allocation, it is our responsibility to release the space when it is not required. The release of storage space becomes important when the storage is limited. When we no longer need the data we stored in a block of memory and we do not intend to use that block for storing any other information, we may release that block of memory for future use, using the free function.

```
free(ptr);
```

ptr is a pointer that has been created by using malloc or calloc.

10.11 To Alter the Size of Allocated Memory

The memory allocated by using calloc or malloc might be insufficient or excess sometimes in both the situations we can change the memory size already allocated with the help of the function realloc. This process is called reallocation of memory. The general statement of reallocation of memory is :

```
Ptr=realloc(ptr,newsize);
```

This function allocates new memory space of size newsize to the pointer variable ptr ans returns a pointer to the first byte of the memory block. The allocated new block may be or may not be at the same region.

Example program for reallocation

```
#include< stdio.h >
#include< stdlib.h >
define NULL 0
main()
{
char *buffer;
/*Allocating memory*/
if((buffer=(char *) malloc(10))==NULL)
{
printf("Malloc failed\n");
exit(1);
```

```
}
printf("Buffer of size %d created \n,_msize(buffer));
strcpy(buffer,"Bangalore");
printf("\nBuffer contains:%s\n",buffer);
/*Reallocation*/
if((buffer=(char *)realloc(buffer,15))==NULL)
{
printf("Reallocation failed\n");
exit(1);
}
printf("\nBuffer size modified.\n");
printf("\nBuffer still contains: %s\n",buffer);
strcpy(buffer,"Mysore");
printf("\nBuffer now contains:%s\n",buffer);
/*freeing memory*/
free(buffer);
}
```

Program 10.1

addresses.c — Playing with addresses of variables and their contents:
* what is done by C with variables, addresses, and values.

```
#include <stdio.h>
void moo(int a, int * b);
int main(void)
    {
    int x;
    int *y;
    x=1;
    y=&x;
    printf("Address of x = %d, value of x = %d\n", &x, x);
    printf("Address of y = %d, value of y = %d, value of *y = %d\n", &y, y, *y);
    moo(9,y);
    }
void moo(int a, int *b)
```

```
        {
        printf("Address of a = %d, value of a = %d\n", &a, a);
        printf("Address of b = %d, value of b = %d, value of *b = %d\n", &b, b, *b);
        }
Output from running this program on my computer:
Address of x = 536869640, value of x = 1
Address of y = 536869632, value of y = 536869640, value of *y = 1
Address of a = 536869608, value of a = 9
Address of b = 536869600, value of b = 536869640, value of *b = 1
```

Program 10.2

cpintarray.c — Example showing how addresses and arrays are alike

```
#include <stdio.h>
#define SIZE 8
void cpIntArray(int *a, int *b, int n)
/*It copies n integers starting at b into a*/
        {
        for(;n>0;n—)
            *a++=*b++;
        }
void printIntArray(int a[], int n)
        /* n is the number of elements in the array a.
         * These values are printed out, five per line. */
        {
        int i;
        for (i=0; i<n; )
            {
            printf("\t%d", a[i++]);
            if (i%5==0)
                printf("\n");
            }
        printf("\n");
        }
int getIntArray(int a[], int nmax, int sentinel)
```

```
/* It reads up to nmax integers and stores then in a; sentinel
 * terminates input. */
{
int n = 0;
int temp;
    do {
    printf("Enter integer [%d to terminate] : ", sentinel);
    scanf("%d", &temp);
    if (temp==sentinel) break;
    if (n==nmax)
        printf("array is full\n");
    else
        a[n++] = temp;
    }while (1);
return n;
}
int main(void)
{
int x[SIZE], nx;
int y[SIZE], ny;
printf("Read the x array:\n");
nx = getIntArray(x,SIZE,0);
printf("The x array is:\n");
printIntArray(x,nx);
printf("Read the y array:\n");
ny = getIntArray(y,SIZE,0);
printf("The y array is:\n");
printIntArray(y,ny);
cpIntArray(x+2,y+3,4);
/*Notice the expression 'x+2'. x is interpreted as the address for the beginning
of the x array. +2 sais to increment that address by two units, in accordance with
the type of x, which is an integer array. Thus we move from x to two integer
locations past it, that is to the location of x[2]. The same reasoning applied to
'y+3'. */
printf("Printing x after having copied 4 elements\n"
    "from y starting at y[3] into x starting at x[2]\n");
```

```
        printIntArray(x,nx);
        }
Here is the interaction in a run of this program:
Read the x array:
Enter integer [0 to terminate] : 1
Enter integer [0 to terminate] : 3
Enter integer [0 to terminate] : 5
Enter integer [0 to terminate] : 7
Enter integer [0 to terminate] : 9
Enter integer [0 to terminate] : 11
Enter integer [0 to terminate] : 13
Enter integer [0 to terminate] : 15
Enter integer [0 to terminate] : 0
The x array is:
    1     3     5     7     9
    11    13    15
Read the y array:
Enter integer [0 to terminate] : 2
Enter integer [0 to terminate] : 4
Enter integer [0 to terminate] : 6
Enter integer [0 to terminate] : 8
Enter integer [0 to terminate] : 10
Enter integer [0 to terminate] : 12
Enter integer [0 to terminate] : 14
Enter integer [0 to terminate] : 16
Enter integer [0 to terminate] : 0
The y array is:
    2     4     6     8     10
    12    14    16
Printing x after having copied 4 elements
from y starting at y[3] into x starting at x[2]
    1     3     8     10    12
    14    13    15
```

11

STRUCTURES AND UNIONS

OBJECTIVE

In this chapter you will learn about C Programming - Structures, Initializing structure, Functions and structures, Passing structure as elements to functions, Passing entire function to functions, Arrays of structure, Structure within a structure and Union.

11.1 What is a Structure?

- Structure is a method of packing the data of different types.
- When we require using a collection of different data items of different data types in that situation we can use a structure.
- A structure is used as a method of handling a group of related data items of different data types.

Syntax of Using Structure

structure definition general format:

```
struct tag_name
{
data type member1;
data type member2;
....
...
}
```

Example of Using Structure:

```
struct lib_books
{
char title[20];
char author[15];
int pages;
float price;
};
```

To holds the details of four fields namely title, author pages and price, the keyword struct declares a structure. These are the members of the structures. Each member may belong to same or different data type. The tag name can be used to define the objects that have the tag names structure. The structure we just declared is not a variable by itself but a template for the structure. We can declare the structure variables using the tag name anywhere in the program. For example the statement, struct lib_books book1,book2,book3; declares the book1,book2,book3 as variables of type struct lib_books each declaration has four elements of the structure lib_books.

The complete structure declaration might look like this

```
struct lib_books
{
char title[20];
char author[15];
int pages;
float price;
};struct lib_books, book1, book2, book3;
```

The following program shows the use of structure

Example program for using a structure

```
#include< stdio.h >
int main()
{
int id_no;
char name[20];
char address[20];
char combination[3];
int age;
}newstudent;
printf("Enter the student information");
printf("Now Enter the student id_no");
scanf("%d",&newstudent.id_no);
printf("Enter the name of the student");
scanf("%s",&new student.name);
printf("Enter the address of the student");
scanf("%s",&new student.address);printf("Enter the cmbination of the student");
scanf("%d",&new student.combination);printf(Enter the age of the student");
scanf("%d",&new student.age);
printf("Student information\n");
printf("student id_number=%d\n",newstudent.id_no);
printf("student name=%s\n",newstudent.name);
printf("student Address=%s\n",newstudent.address);
printf("students combination=%s\n",newstudent.combination);
printf("Age of student=%d\n",newstudent.age);
}
```

11.2 Giving Values to Members

As mentioned earlier the members themselves are not variables they should be linked to structure variables in order to make them meaningful members. The link between a member and a variable is established using the member operator '.' Which is known as dot operator or period operator.

For example:

Book1.price

Is the variable representing the price of book1 and can be treated like any other ordinary variable. We can use scanf statement to assign values like

scanf("%s",book1.file);

scanf("%d",& book1.pages);

Or we can assign variables to the members of book1

book1.price=288.50;

Example program for using a structure

```
#include< stdio.h >
int main()
{
int id_no;
char name[20];
char address[20];
char combination[3];
int age;
}newstudent;
printf("Enter the student information");
printf("Now Enter the student id_no");
scanf("%d",&newstudent.id_no);
printf("Enter the name of the student");
scanf("%s",&new student.name);
printf("Enter the address of the student");
scanf("%s",&new student.address);
printf("Enter the cmbination of the student");
scanf("%d",&new student.combination);
printf("Enter the age of the student");
scanf("%d",&new student.age);
printf("Student information\n");
printf("student id_number=%d\n",newstudent.id_no);
printf("student name=%s\n",newstudent.name);
printf("student Address=%s\n",newstudent.address);
printf("students combination=%s\n",newstudent.combination);
printf("Age of student=%d\n",newstudent.age);
}
```

11.3 Initializing Structure

Like other data type we can initialize structure when we declare them. As for initalization goes structure obeys the same set of rules as arrays we initalize the fields of a structure by the following structure declaration with a list containing values for weach fileds as with arrays these values must be evaluate at compile time.

Example:

```
Struct student newstudent
{
12345,
"Sachin"
"bharati Vidyapeeth";
"Computer";
25;
};
```

this initializes the id_no field to 12345, the name field to "Sachin", the address field to "Bharati vidyapeeth" the field combination to "Computer" and the age field to 25.

11.4 Functions and Structures

We can pass structures as arguments to functions. Unlike array names however, which always point to the start of the array, structure names are not pointers. As a result, when we change structure parameter inside a function, we do not effect its corresponding argument.

11.4.1 Passing structure to elements to functions

A structure may be passed into a function as individual member or a separate variable. A program example to display the contents of a structure passing the individual elements to a function is shown below.

```
# include < stdio.h >
void main()
{
int emp_id;
char name[25];
char department[10];
float salary;
};
```

```
static struct emp1={125,"sampath","operator",7500.00};
/* pass only emp_id and name to display function*/
display(emp1.emp_id,emp1.name);
}
/* function to display structure variables*/
display(e_no,e_name)
int e_no,e_name;
{
printf("%d%s",e_no,e_name);
}
```

in the declaration of structure type, emp_id and name have been declared as integer and character array. When we call the function display() using display(emp1.emp_id,emp1.name); we are sending the emp_id and name to function display(0); it can be immediately realized that to pass individual elements would become more tedious as the number of structure elements go on increasing a better way would be to pass the entire structure variable at a time.

11.4.2 Passing entire structure to functions

In case of structures having to having numerous structure elements passing these individual elements would be a tedious task. In such cases we may pass whole structure to a function as shown below:

```
# include stdio.h>
{
int emp_id;
char name[25];
char department[10];
float salary;
};

void main()
{
static struct employee emp1=
{
12,
"sadanand",
"computer",
7500.00
};
```

```
/*sending entire employee structure*/
display(emp1);
}
/*function to pass entire structure variable*/
display(empf)
struct employee empf
{
printf("%d%s,%s,%f", empf.empid,empf.name,empf.department,empf.salary);
}
```

11.5 Arrays of Structure

It is possible to define a array of structures for example if we are maintaining information of all the students in the college and if 100 students are studying in the college. We need to use an array than single variables. We can define an array of structures as shown in the following example:

```
#include< stdio.h >
{
struct info
{
int id_no;
char name[20];
char address[20];
char combination[3];
int age;
}
struct info std[100];
int I,n;
printf("Enter the number of students");
scanf("%d",&n);
printf(" Enter Id_no,name address combination age\m");
for(I=0;I < n;I++)
scanf(%d%s%s%s%d",&std[I].id_no,std[I].name,std[I].address,std[I].
combination,&std[I].age);
printf("\n Student information");
for (I=0;I< n;I++)
printf("%d%s%s%s%d\n",
",std[I].id_no,std[I].name,std[I].address,std[I].combination,std[I].age);
}
```

11.6 Structure within a Structure

A structure may be defined as a member of another structure. In such structures the declaration of the embedded structure must appear before the declarations of other structures.

```
struct date
{
int day;
int month;
int year;
};
struct student
{
int id_no;
char name[20];
char address[20];
char combination[3];
int age;
structure date def;
structure date doa;
}oldstudent, newstudent;
```

the structure student contains another structure date as one of its members.

11.7 Union

However the members that we compose a union all share the same storage area within the computers memory whereas each member within a structure is assigned its own unique storage area. Thus unions are used to observe memory. They are useful for the application involving multiple members. Where values need not be assigned to all the members at any time. Union like structure contain members whose individual data types may differ from one another also. Like structures union can be declared using the keyword union as follows:

```
union item
{
int m;
float p;
char c;
}code;
```

this declares a variable code of type union item. The union contains three members each with a different data type. However we can use only one of them at a time. This is because if only one location is allocated for union variable irrespective of size. The compiler allocates a piece of storage that is large enough to access a union member we can use the same syntax that we use to access structure members, i.e.,

code.m

code.p

code.c

are all valid member variables. During accessing we should make sure that we are accessing the member whose value is currently stored.

For example a statement such as

code.m=456;

code.p=456.78;

printf("%d",code.m);

Would produce erroneous result.

In effect a union creates a storage location that can be used by one of its members at a time. When a different number is assigned a new value the new value supercedes the previous members value. Unions may be used in all places where a structure is allowed. The notation for accessing a union member that is nested inside a structure remains the same as for the nested structure.

Program 11.1

enum1.c — Starting to use enumerated types: Printing for each day of the week, today, yesterday, and tomorrow, both as a string and as a number.

```
#include <stdio.h>
/* Introducing an enumerated data type */
enum days {monday,tuesday,wednesday,thursday,friday,saturday,sunday};
typedef enum days days; /* This allows us to use "days" as an abbreviation
                for "enum days" */
/* Two useful functions */
days yesterday(days today)
   {
   return (today+6)%7;
   }
days tomorrow(days today)
   {
   return (today+1)%7;
```

```
}
/* A useful array: thedays is an array of constant (i.e you cannot
   modify them) pointers to constant (i.e. you cannot modify them) strings */
const char * const thedays[] =
                {"monday", "tuesday", "wednesday", "thursday",
                 "friday", "saturday", "sunday"};
int main(void)
  {
  days today;
  printf("today   \tyesterday  \ttomorrow\n"
  printf("=========================================\n");
  for (today=monday;today<=sunday;today++)
         printf("%s = %d \t %s = %d \t %s = %d\n",
            thedays[today], today, thedays[yesterday(today)],
            yesterday(today), thedays[tomorrow(today)],
            tomorrow(today));
  }
```

The output is:

```
today             yesterday         tomorrow
==================================================
monday = 0        sunday = 6        tuesday = 1
tuesday = 1       monday = 0        wednesday = 2
wednesday = 2     tuesday = 1       thursday = 3
thursday = 3      wednesday = 2     friday = 4
friday = 4        thursday = 3      saturday = 5
saturday = 5      friday = 4        sunday = 6
sunday = 6        saturday = 5      monday = 0
```

Program 11.2

enum2.c — Starting to use enumerated types: Printing for each day of the week, today, yesterday, and tomorrow, both as a string and as a number. We use typedef

```
#include <stdio.h>
/* Introducing an enumerated data type */
typedef enum {monday,tuesday,wednesday,thursday,friday,saturday,sunday} days;
/* Two useful functions */
days yesterday(days today);
days tomorrow(days today);
char *thedays[] = {"monday", "tuesday", "wednesday", "thursday",
            "friday", "saturday", "sunday"};
int main(void)
    {
    days today;
    printf("today   \tyesterday  \ttomorrow\n"
    printf("==========================================\n");
    for (today=monday;today<=sunday;today++)
        printf("%s = %d \t %s = %d \t %s = %d\n",
            thedays[today], today, thedays[yesterday(today)],
            yesterday(today), thedays[tomorrow(today)],
            tomorrow(today));
    }
days yesterday(days today)
    {
    return (today+6)%7;
    }
days tomorrow(days today)
    {
    return (today+1)%7;
    }
The output is:
today              yesterday          tomorrow
==========================================
monday = 0         sunday = 6         tuesday = 1
tuesday = 1        monday = 0         wednesday = 2
wednesday = 2      tuesday = 1        thursday = 3
thursday = 3       wednesday = 2      friday = 4
friday = 4         thursday = 3       saturday = 5
saturday = 5       friday = 4         sunday = 6
sunday = 6         saturday = 5       monday = 0
```

Program 11.3

struct.c - Simple uses of structures

```
#include <stdio.h>
struct student {
      int  mid;
      int final;
      int hmws;
};

void main(void)
        {
        struct student sam = {85, 90, 88};
        struct student tom = {93, 88, 91};
        struct student *he = &tom;  /* We can access a structure and its fields
                               through a pointer */
We cannot read or write directly a studentas we can integers, and reals, etc.
Also, we cannot compare directly two students
        (i.e. we cannot say (sam == tom)].
But we can assign a student to another student.
        For example:   tom = sam;
Then we can output the value of tom by printing its various fields:
        printf("tom = {%d, %d, %d}\n",  tom.mid, tom.final, tom.hmws);
Notice the dot notation for accessing the fields, of tom.
The output will be tom = {85, 90, 88}
        printf("*he = {%d, %d, %d}\n",  he->mid, he->final, he->hmws);
Notice the arrow notation for accessing the fields from he.
The output will be *he = {85, 90, 88}
We would get the same output if we access the fields in a different way:
        printf("*he = {%d, %d, %d}\n",  (*he).mid, (*he).final, (*he).hmws);
        }
```

Program 11.4

```
#include <stdio.h>
#include <string.h>
#include <stdlib.h>
#define SIZE 50
#define MAX 10
 typedef struct node
    {
    char symbol[MAX];
     int value;
     struct node *next;
   } entry;
  typedef entry *entry_ptr;
int hash_value(char * name)
    {
    int sum=0;
    while( *name != '\0')
        {
        sum += *name;
        name++;
        }
    return(sum % SIZE);
  }
void initialize( entry_ptr table[])
    {
    int i=0;
    for(i=0; i<SIZE; i++)
        table[i] = NULL;
    }
void insert( entry_ptr table[], char *name, int val)
    {
    int h, flag = 1;
    entry_ptr temp;
    h = hash_value(name);
    temp = table[h];
    while(  temp != NULL && flag )
```

```
            {
            if( strcmp(temp->symbol,name) == 0)
                {
                        printf("The symbol %s is already present in the
                    table\n",name);
                flag =0;;
                }
            temp=temp->next;
            }
        if(flag)
            {
            temp = (entry_ptr) malloc(sizeof( entry));
            if(temp == NULL)
            {
                printf("ERRRR .......\n");
                exit(0);
                }
            strcpy(temp->symbol,name);
            temp->value = val;
            temp->next = table[h];
            table[h]=temp;
            }
        }
    void retrieve( entry_ptr table[],char *name)
        {
        int h,flag =1;
      entry_ptr temp;
      h = hash_value(name);
      temp = table[h];
      while( temp != NULL && flag)
            {
            if( strcmp(temp->symbol,name) == 0)
            {
            printf("The symbol %s is  present in the table and having
                    value = %d\n",name,temp->value);
                flag =0;
```

```
            }
        temp=temp->next;
        }
    if(flag == 1)
    printf("The symbol %s is not present in the table \n",name);
    }
void main()
    {
    entry_ptr table[SIZE];
    char name[MAX];
    int value,n;
    initialize(table);
        do
        {
            do
            {
            printf("Enter the symbol and value pair to be
                inserted\n");
            scanf("%s %d",name,&value);
            insert(table,name,value);
            printf("Enter 1 to continue\n");
            scanf("%d",&n);
            }while(n == 1);
        do
            {
            printf("Enter the symbol whose value is to be
                retrieved\n");
            scanf("%s",name);
            retrieve(table,name);
            printf("Enter 1 to continue\n");
            scanf("%d",&n);
            }while( n == 1);
        printf("Eneter 1 to continue\n");
        scanf("%d",&n);
        }while(n == 1);
    }
```

Program 11.5

List Implementation Using Array

```
#include<stdio.h>
#include<conio.h>
#define MAX 20 //maximum no of elements in the list
//user defined datatypes
struct
{
    int list[MAX];
    int element;          //new element to be inserted
    int pos;              //position of the element to be inserted or deleted
    int length;           //total no of elements
}l;
enum boolean { true, false };
typedef enum boolean boolean;

/* function prototypes */
int menu(void);              /* function to display the list of operations */
void create(void);           /* function to create initial set of elements */
void insert(int, int);       /* function to insert the given element at specified position */
void delet(int);             /* function to delete the element at given position */
void find(int);              /* function to find the position of the given element, if exists */
void display(void);          /* function to display the elements in the list */
boolean islistfull(void);    /* function to check whether the list is full or not */
boolean islistempty(void);   /* function to check whether the list is empty or not */

void main()
{
    int ch;
    int element;
    int pos;
    l.length = 0;
    while(1)
        {
        ch = menu();
```

```
switch (ch)
  {
  case 1:
    l.length = 0;
    create();
    break;
  case 2:
    if (islistfull() != true)
          {
          printf("\tEnter the New element : ");
          scanf("%d", &element);
          printf("\tEnter the Position : ");
          scanf("%d", &pos);
          insert(element, pos);
          }
    else
          {
          printf("\tList if Full. Cannot insert");
          printf("\nPress any key to continue...");
          getch();
          }
    break;
  case 3:
    if (islistempty() != true)
          {
          printf("Enter the position of element to be
                deleted : ");
          scanf("%d", &pos);
          delet(pos);
          }
    else
          {
          printf("List is Empty.");
          printf("\nPress any key to continue...");
          getch();
```

```
                    }
                break;
            case 4:
                printf("No of elements in the list is %d", l.length);
                printf("\nPress any key to continue...");
                getch();
                break;
            case 5:
                printf("Enter the element to be searched : ");
                scanf("%d", &element);
                find(element);
                break;
            case 6:
                display();
                break;
            case 7:
                exit(0);
                break;
            default:
                printf("Invalid Choice");
                printf("\nPress any key to continue...");
                getch();
        }
    }
}

/* function to display the list of elements */
int menu()
{
    int ch;
    clrscr();
    printf("\n\t\t\t**********************************************\n");
    printf("\t\t******LIST Implementation Using Arrays******\n");
    printf("\t\t**********************************************\n\n");
    printf("\t1. Create\n\t2. Insert\n\t3. Delete\n\t4. Count\n\t5. Find\n\t6.
```

```
        display\n\t7. Exit\n\n\tEnter your choice : ");
    scanf("%d", &ch);
    printf("\n\n");
    return ch;
}
/* function to create initial set of elements */
void create(void)
{
    int element;
    int flag=1;
    while(flag==1)
        {
        printf("Enter an element : ");
        scanf("%d", &element);
        l.list[l.length] = element;
        l.length++;
        printf("To insert another element press '1' : ");
        scanf("%d", &flag);
        }
}
/* function to display the elements in the list */
void display(void)
{
    int i;
    for (i=0; i<l.length; i++)
        printf("Element %d : %d \n", i+1, l.list[i]);
    printf("Press any key to continue...");
    getch();
}
/* function to insert the given element at specified position */
void insert(int element, int pos)
{
    int i;
    if (pos == 0)
        {
```

```
            printf("\n\nCannot insert at zeroth position");
            getch();
            return;
            }
        if (pos-1 > l.length)
            {
            printf("\n\nOnly %d elements exit. Cannot insert at %d postion",
                        l.length, pos);
            printf("\nPress any key to continue...");
            getch();
            }
        else
            {
            for (i=l.length; i>=pos-1; i—)
                {
                l.list[i+1] = l.list[i];
                }
            l.list[pos-1] = element;
            l.length++;
            }
    }
    /* function to delete the element at given position */
    void delet(int pos)
    {
        int i;
        if(pos == 0)
            {
            printf("\n\nCannot delete at zeroth position");
            getch();
            return;
            }
        if (pos > l.length)
            {
            printf("\n\nOnly %d elements exit. Cannot delete", l.length, pos);
            printf("\nPress any key to continue...");
```

```
        getch();
        return;
        }
    for (i=pos-1; i<l.length; i++)
        {
        l.list[i] = l.list[i+1];
        }
    l.length—;
}
/* function to find the position of the given element, if exists */
void find(int element)
{
    int i;
    int flag = 1;
    for (i=0; i<l.length; i++)
        {
        if(l.list[i] == element)
            {
            printf ("%d exists at %d position",element, i+1);
            flag = 0;
            printf("\nPress any key to continue...");
            getch();
            break;
            }
        }
    if(flag == 1)
        {
        printf("Element not found.\nPress any key to continue...");
        getch();
        }
}
/* function to check whether the list is full or not */
boolean islistfull(void)
{
    if (l.length == MAX)
```

```
        return true;
    else
        return false;
}
/* function to check whether the list is empty or not */
boolean islistempty(void)
{
    if (l.length == 0)
        return true;
    else
        return false;
}
```

Sample Output:

```
1. Create
2. Insert
3. Delete
4. Count
5. Find
6. Display
7. Exit

Enter your Choice: 1
Enter an element: 25
To insert another element press 1: 1

Enter an element: 50
To insert another element press 1: 0

Enter your Choice: 6
Element in the List are
1. 25
2. 50

Enter your Choice: 2
Enter an element: 5
```

```
Enter the position: 1
Element in the List are
1. 25
2. 50

Enter your Choice: 3
Enter the position: 3

Enter your Choice: 6
Element in the List are
1. 5
2. 25

Enter your Choice: 4
Number of Elements: 2

Enter your Choice: 7
```

■■■

12

File Management

Objective

In this chapter you will learn about - File Handling in C, File operation functions , Defining and opening a file, Closing a file, The getw and putw functions, The fprintf & fscanf functions, Random access to files, fseek function and Command line argument.

12.1 Introduction

C supports a number of functions that have the ability to perform basic file operations.

(1) Naming a file

(2) Opening a file

(3) Reading from a file

(4) Writing data into a file

(5) Closing a file

In case of large volume of data the console oriented I/O operations have some limitations such as, It becomes time consuming to handle large volumes of data through terminals. The entire data is lost when either the program is terminated or computer is turned off therefore it is necessary to store data on the disks and read whenever necessary, without destroying the data. This method employs the concept of files to store data.

12.2 File Operation Functions in C

The some functions are important to operate on the file these are given in following table

Function Name	Operation
Fopen()	Creates a new file for use Opens a new existing file for use
Fclose()	Closes a file which has been opened for use
getc()	Reads a character from a file
putc()	Writes a character to a file
fprintf()	Writes a set of data values to a file
fscanf()	Reads a set of data values from a file
getw()	Reads a integer from a file
putw()	Writes an integer to the file
Fseek()	Sets the position to a desired point in the file
ftell()	Gives the current position in the file
rewind()	Sets the position to the beginning of the file

12.2.1 Defining and opening a file

If we want to store data in a file into the secondary memory, we must specify the filename, data structure, purpose.

The general format of the function used for opening a file is

```
FILE *fp;
fp=fopen("filename","mode");
```

The first statement declares the variable fp as a pointer to the data type FILE. File is a structure that is defined in the I/O Library. The second statement opens the file named filename and assigns an identifier to the FILE type pointer fp. The second statement also specifies the mode

R - Open the file for read only.

W - Open the file for writing only.

A - Open the file for appending data to it.

The file <stdio.h> contains declarations for the Standard I/O library and should always be included at the very beginning of C programs using files. Constants such as FILE, EOF and NULL are defined in <stdio.h>.You should note that a file pointer is simply a variable like an integer or character. It does not point to a file or the data in a file. It is simply used to indicate which file your I/O operation refers to. A file number is used in the Basic language and a unit number is used in FORTRAN for the same purpose. The function fopen is one of the Standard Library functions and returns a file pointer which you use to refer to the file you have opened e.g.

```
fp = fopen( "prog.c", "r") ;
```

The above statement opens a file called prog.c for reading and associates the file pointer fp with the file.

12.2.2 Closing a file:

The input output library supports the function to close a file; it is in the following format.

```
fclose(file_pointer);
```

A file must be closed as soon as all operations on it have been completed. This would close the file associated with the file pointer.

```
....
FILE *fp1 *fp2;
fp1=fopen ("Input","w");
fp2=fopen ("Output","r");
....
...
fclose(fp1);
fclose(fp2)
```

The above program opens two files and closes them after all operations on them are completed, once a file is closed its file pointer can be reversed on other file.

12.3 File I/O

12.3.1 The getc and putc functions

The Standard I/O Library provides similar routines for file I/O to those used for standard I/O. The routine getc(fp) is similar to getchar() and putc(c,fp) is similar to putchar(c).

Thus the statement

```
c = getc(fp);
```

reads the next character from the file referenced by fp and the statement

```
putc(c,fp);
```

writes the character c into file referenced by fp.

file.c: Display contents of a file on screen

```
#include <stdio.h>
void main()
{
    FILE *fopen(), *fp;
    int c ;
    fp = fopen( "prog.c", "r" );
if (hFile == NULL)
{
/* Error, file not found */
}
Else
        {
        c = getc( fp ) ;
    while (  c != EOF )
            {
            putchar( c );
            c = getc ( fp );
            }
        }
    fclose( fp );
}
```

In this program, we open the file prog.c for reading. We then read a character from the file. This file must exist for this program to work. If the file is empty, we are at the end, so getc returns EOF a special value to indicate that the end of file has been reached. (Normally -1 is used for EOF)The while loop simply keeps reading characters from the file and displaying them, until the end of the file is reached. The function fclose is used to close the file i.e. indicate that we are finished processing this file.

12.3.2 The getw and putw functions

These are integer-oriented functions. They are similar to get c and putc functions and are used to read and write integer values. These functions would be usefull when we deal with only integer data. The general forms of getw and putw are:

```
putw(integer,fp);
getw(fp);
```

Example program for using getw and putw functions

```
#include< stdio.h >
main()
{
FILE *f1,*f2,*f3;
int number I;
printf("Contents of the data file\n\n");
f1=fopen("prog.c","W");
for(I=1;I< 30;I++)
{
scanf("%d",&number);
if(number==-1)
break;
putw(number,f1);
}
fclose(f1);
f1=fopen("prog.c","r");
f2=fopen("odd.txt","w");
f3=fopen("even.txt","w");
while((number=getw(f1))!=EOF)/* Read from data file*/
{
if(number%2==0)
putw(number,f3);/*Write to even file*/
else
putw(number,f2);/*write to odd file*/
}
fclose(f1);
fclose(f2);
fclose(f3);
f2=fopen("odd.txt","r");
f3=fopen("even.txt","r");
printf("\n\n Contents of the odd file\n\n");
while(number=getw(f2))!=EOF)
printf("%d%d",number);
printf("\n\n Contents of the even file");
while(number=getw(f3))!=EOF)
printf("%d",number);
fclose(f2);
fclose(f3);
}
```

Write a program to combine contents of two files in a third file. Add line number at the beginning of each line.

```
# include <stdio.h>
# include <conio.h>
# include <process.h>
void main()
{
FILE *f1,*f2,*f3;
char ch;
int n=1;
clrscr();
f1=fopen("text1.txt","r");
f2=fopen ("text2.txt","r");
f3=fopen ("text3.txt","w");
if (f1==NULL || f2==NULL || f3==NULL)
{
printf ("error in file opening");
exit(1);
}
putw(n,f3);
while (!feof(f1))
{
ch=fgetc(f1);
fputc(ch,f3);
if (ch=='\n')
{
n++;
putw(n,f3);
}
}
while (!feof(f2))
{
ch=fgetc(f2);
fputc(ch,f3);
if (ch=='\n')
```

```
{
n++;
fputc(n,f3);
}
}
fcloseall();
f3=fopen ("text3.txt","r");
printf ("%d ", getw(f3));
while (!feof(f3))
{
ch=fgetc(f3);
printf ("%c ",ch);
if (ch=='\n')
printf ("%d ",getw (f3));
}
}
OUTPUT
1 abcdefghijklmnopq
2
3 afajfgfggf
```

Explanation In the above program three files are opened. Two files "text2.txt" and "text2.txt" are opened in read mode and "text2.txt" is opened in write mode. One by one, contents of both the file is read and written in the file"text2.txt." When carriage return occurs using putw() line number is inserted at the starting of each line. While reading the contents of file using getw () function line number is read and displayed.

12.3.3 The fprintf & fscanf functions

The fprintf and scanf functions are identical to printf and scanf functions except that they work on files. The first argument of these functions is a file pointer which specifies the file to be used.

12.3.3.1 The general format of fprintf is

fprintf(fp,"control string", list);

Where fp is a file pointer associated with a file that has been opened for writing. The control string is file output specifications list may include variable, constant and string.

fprintf(f1,%s%d%f",name,age,7.5);

Here name is an array variable of type char and age is an int variable

12.3.3.2 The general format of fscanf is

fscanf(fp,"controlstring",list);

This statement would cause the reading of items in the control string.

Like scanf, fscanf also returns the number of items that are successfully read.

fscanf(f2,"5s%d",item,&quantity");

Sample Program to Open a File for Reading

```
#include <stdio.h>
int main() {
FILE *fp; // declare a FILE pointer
fp = fopen("data.txt", "r");
/* open a text file for reading */
if(fp==NULL) {
printf("Error: failed to open file.\n");
return 1;
}
Else
{
printf("File successfully opened\n");
fscanf(fp, "%d", &data);
/* read an integer from the file */
fclose(fp);
return 0;
}
}
```

Sample Program to Open a File for Writing

```
#include <stdio.h>
int main() {
FILE *fp; /* declare a FILE pointer */
file = fopen("data/writing.txt", "w");
/* create a text file for writing */
if(fp==NULL) {
printf("Error: can't create file.\n");
return 1;
```

```
}
Else
{
printf("File created\n");
/* write an integer to the file */
fprintf(fp, "%d\n", 10);
fclose(fp);
return 0;
}
}
```

Program to handle mixed data types

```
#include< stdio.h >
main()
{
FILE *fp;
int num,qty,I;
float price, value;
char item[10],filename[10];
printf("Input filename");
scanf("%s",filename);
fp=fopen(filename,"w");
printf("Input inventory data\n\n"0;
printf("Item name number price quantity\n");
for I=1;I< =3;I++)
{
fscanf(stdin,"%s%d%f%d",item,&number,&price,&quality);
fprintf(fp,"%s%d%f%d",itemnumber,price,quality);
}
fclose (fp);
fprintf(stdout,"\n\n");
fp=fopen(filename,"r");
printf("Item name number price quantity value");
for(I=1;I< =3;I++)
{
```

```
fscanf(fp,"%s%d%f%d",item,&number,&prince,&quality);
value=price*quantity");
fprintf("stdout,"%s%d%f%d%d\n",item,number,price,quantity,value);
}
fclose(fp);
}
```

Other Options When Opening Files

The following four options are important:

"a" lets you open a text file for appending - i.e., add data to the end of the current text.

"r+" will open a text file to read from or write to.

"w+" will create a text file to read from or write to.

"a+" will either create or open a text file for appending.

12.4 Command Line Parameters: Arguments to main()

Accessing the command line arguments is a very useful facility. It takes the argument "prog.c" and opens a file with that name, which it then displays. The command line arguments include the command name itself to access these arguments from within a C program, you pass parameters to the function main (). The use of arguments to main is a key feature of many C programs.

The declaration of main looks like this:

```
int main (int argc,  char *argv[])
```

This declaration states that

(1) main returns an integer value (used to determine if the program terminates successfully)

(2) argc is the number of command line arguments including the command itself, i.e., argc must be at least 1

(3) argv is an array of the command line arguments

The declaration of argv means that it is an array of pointers to strings. By the normal rules about arguments whose type is array, what actually gets passed to main is the address of the first element of the array. As a result, an equivalent declaration is:

```
int main (int argc,  char **argv)
```

When the program starts, the following conditions hold true:

0 argc is greater than 0.

0 argv [argc] is a null pointer.

0 argv[0], argv[1], ..., argv[argc-1] are pointers to strings
with implementation defined meanings.

o argv[0] is a string which contains the program's name, or is an empty string if the name isn't available. Remaining members of argv are the program's arguments.

Program 12.1

print_args.c: Echo command line arguments

```
#include <stdio.h>
#include <stdlib.h>
int main(int argc,  char *argv[])
{
    int i = 0 ;
    int num_args ;
    num_args = argc;
    While (num_args > 0)
        {
        printf (“%s\n“, argv[i]);
        i++ ;
        Num_args—;
        }
}
```

If the name of this program is print_args, an example of its execution is as follows:

```
print_args Hello Welcome Renushe
print_args
Hello
Welcome
Renushe
```

Program 12.2

counts.c – It contains a program that is given as command parameter the name of a text file, say, temp.dat. It will read each line of temp.dat and print out in correspondence the number of characters and words on that line. At the end it will print out the number of lines that were read.

```
#include <stdio.h>
int main (int argc, char *argv[])
    {
    FILE *fp;
    int nchars, nwords, nlines;
    int lastnblank;    /* 0 iff the last character was a space */
    char c;
    if(argc!=2)
        {
        printf("Usage: %s filename\n", argv[0]);
        exit(0);
        }
    if((fp=fopen(argv[1],"r"))==NULL)
        {
        perror("fopen");
        exit(0);
        }
    nchars=nwords=nlines=lastnblank=0;
    while((c=getc(fp))!=EOF)
        {
        nchars++;
        if (c=='\n')
            {
            if (lastnblank)
            nwords++;
            printf("words=%d, characters=%d\n", nwords, nchars);
            nchars=nwords=lastnblank=0;
            nlines++;
            }
        else
            {
            if (((c==' ')||(c=='\t'))&(lastnblank))
                nwords++;
            lastnblank=((c!=' ')&&(c!='\t'));
            }
        }
    printf("lines=%d\n", nlines);
    fclose(fp);
    }
```

Program 12.3

cpfile.c — Similar to Unix's cp command.
This program will be called with two parameters,
the names of two files. It copies the first to the second.

```
#include <stdio.h>
#include <stdlib.h>
int main(int argc, char * argv[])
  {
  FILE *fin, *fout;
  char c;
  if (argc!=3)
    {
    printf("Usage: %s filein fileout\n", argv[0]);
    exit(0);
    }
  if ((fin=fopen(argv[1],"r"))==NULL)
    {
    perror("fopen filein");
    exit(0);
    }
  if ((fout=fopen(argv[2],"w"))==NULL)
    {
    perror("fopen fileout");
    exit(0);
    }
  while ((c=getc(fin))!=EOF)
        putc(c,fout);
  fclose(fin);
  fclose(fout);
  return 0;
  }
```

Program 12.4

studentarray.c – Reads a file containing a sequence of records representing students, places them into an array, then writes that array out to a new files. The names of the files are passed in as command line parameters.

```
#include <stdio.h>
#define SIZE 10
#define NAMESIZE 25
typedef struct
   {
   char name[NAMESIZE];
   int  midterm;
   int final;
   int homeworks;
   } student;
void writeStudentArray(char filename[], student a[], int n)
   /* n is the number of elements in the array a.
    * filename is the name of the file where we will
    * write.      */
   {
   FILE *fd;  /* File descriptor used for filename */
   int i;
  if(n<=0)
   return;
   if((fd=fopen(filename,"w"))==NULL)
      {
      perror("fopen");
      exit(1);
      }
   for (i=0;i<n;i++)
      {
      fprintf(fd,"%s %d %d %d\n",
         a->name, a->midterm, a->final, a->homeworks);
      a++;
```

```
        }
    fclose(fd);
    }
int readStudentArray(char filename[], student a[], int nmax)
    /* It reads up to nmax student records
     * from file filename and stores them in a.
     * It returns the number of records actually read. */
    {
    FILE *fd;  /* File descriptor used for filename */
    int i=0;
    if((fd=fopen(filename,"r"))==NULL)
        {
        perror("fopen");
        exit(1);
        }
    while(fscanf(fd,"%s %d %d %d",
          a->name, &a->midterm, &a->final, &a->homeworks)!=EOF)
        {
        if(++i==nmax)break;  /* We have filled up the table */
        a++;
        }
    fclose(fd);
    return i;
    }
int main(int argc, char *argv[])
    {
    int n;
    student table[SIZE];
    if(argc!=3)
        {
        printf("Usage: %s infile outfile\n", argv[0]);
        exit(0);
        }
    n = readStudentArray(argv[1],table,SIZE);
    writeStudentArray(argv[2],table,n);
    }
```

Program 12.5

stringmerge.c — Given two sorted files of strings, it creates a sorted file consisting of all their elements. The names of the files are passed as command line parameters.

```
#include <stdio.h>
#define MAXBUFFER 128
int getline(FILE * fd, char buff[], int nmax)
    {
  /* It reads a line from fd and stores up to nmax of
   * its characters to buff.   */
    char c;
    int n=0;
  while ((c=getc(fd))!='\n')
        {
        if(c==EOF)return EOF;
        if(n<nmax)
            buff[n++]=c;
        }
    buff[n]='\0';
    return n;
    }
int stringMerge(char filename1[], char filename2[] , char filename3[])
    {
  /* Given two sorted files of strings, called filename1 and filename2,
   * it writes their merged sequence to the file filename3.
   * It returns the total number of strings written to filename3.  */
    FILE *fd1, *fd2, *fd3;
    char buffer1[MAXBUFFER], buffer2[MAXBUFFER];
    int ln1, ln2;
    int n=0;
    if ((fd1=fopen(filename1, "r"))==NULL)
        {
        perror("fopen");
        exit(1);
```

```
    }
if ((fd2=fopen(filename2, "r"))==NULL)
    {
    perror("fopen");
    exit(1);
    }
if ((fd3=fopen(filename3, "w"))==NULL)
    {
    perror("fopen");
    exit(1);
    }
ln1 = getline(fd1,buffer1,MAXBUFFER-1);
ln2 = getline(fd2,buffer2,MAXBUFFER-1);
while ((ln1!=EOF) && (ln2!=EOF))
    {
    if (strcmp(buffer1,buffer2)<=0)
        {
        fprintf(fd3, "%s\n", buffer1);
        ln1 = getline(fd1,buffer1,MAXBUFFER-1);
        }
    else
        {
        fprintf(fd3, "%s\n", buffer2);
        ln2 = getline(fd2,buffer2,MAXBUFFER-1);
        }
    n++;
    }
while (ln1!=EOF)
    {
    fprintf(fd3, "%s\n", buffer1);
    ln1=getline(fd1,buffer1,MAXBUFFER-1);
    n++;
    }
while (ln2!=EOF)
    {
```

```
        fprintf(fd3, "%s\n", buffer2);
        ln2=getline(fd2,buffer2,MAXBUFFER-1);
        n++;
        }
    fclose(fd1);
    fclose(fd2);
    fclose(fd3);
    return n;
    }
int main(int argc, char *argv[])
    {
    if(argc!=4)
        {
        printf("Usage: %s sortedfile1 sortedfile2 mergefile\n", argv[0]);
        exit(0);
        }
    printf("We have %d merged records\n",
    stringMerge(argv[1], argv[2], argv[3]));
    }
```

Program 12.6

sortmerge.c - Reads a file containing a sequence of records representing students and places them into an array table1. It does the same for a second file placing result in table2. It then sorts table1 and table2 in non descending order on the basis of their name fields. It now stores the merge of the two sorted sequences in an array table3. Finally it writes the result to a third file.The names of the three files are assed as command line parameters

```
#include <stdio.h>
#define SIZE 10
#define NAMESIZE 25
typedef struct {
  char name[NAMESIZE];
  int  midterm;
  int final;
  int homeworks;
} student;
```

```
void writeStudentArray(char filename[], student a[], int n)
    /* n is the number of elements in the array a.
     * filename is the name of the file where we will
     * write.    */
    {
    FILE *fd;  /* File descriptor used for filename */
    int i;
    if(n<=0)
        return;
    if((fd=fopen(filename,"w"))==NULL)
        {
        perror("fopen");
        exit(1);
        }
    for (i=0;i<n;i++)
        {
        fprintf(fd,"%s %d %d %d\n",
            a->name, a->midterm, a->final, a->homeworks);
        a++;
        }
    fclose(fd);
    }
int readStudentArray(char filename[], student a[], int nmax)
    /* It reads up to nmax student records
     * from file filename and stores them in a.
     * It returns the number of records actually read.
     * WARNING: We assume that the name of the students contain no spaces.  */
    {
    FILE *fd;  /* File descriptor used for filename */
    int i=0;
  if((fd=fopen(filename,"r"))==NULL)
        {
        perror("fopen");
        exit(1);
        }
```

```
    while(fscanf(fd,"%s %d %d %d",
        a->name, &a->midterm, &a->final, &a->homeworks)!=EOF)
        {
        if(++i==nmax)break;  /* We have filled up the table */
        a++;
        }
    fclose(fd);
    return i;
    }
void sortStudentArray(student table[], int n)
    {
  /* It sorts in nondecreasing order on the basis of their
   * names the first n records of table.
   * WARNING: THIS IS A NULL STUB.   */
    }
int mergeStudentArray(student table3[], student table1[], int n1,
            student table2[], int n2)
    {
  /* It merges into table3 the first n1 student records of table1
   * and the first n2 student records of table2. The records in
   * table1 and table2 are sorted in nondecreasing order of their
   * name fields. It returns n1+n2.
   * WARNING: THIS IS A STUB WHERE WE JUST COPY, NOT MERGE.   */
    int i,j=0;
    for(i=0;i<n1;i++)
        {
        table3[j++] = table1[i];
        }
    for(i=0;i<n2;i++)
        {
        table3[j++] = table2[i];
        }
    return n1+n2;
    }
int main(int argc, char *argv[])
```

```
{
int n1,     /* Number of students in first sequence */
n2,       /* Number of students in second sequence */
n3;       /* Number of students in resulting sequence */
student table1[SIZE], /* Students in first sequence */
table2[SIZE],       /* Students in second sequence */
table3[SIZE+SIZE];  /* Students in merged sequence */
if(argc!=4)
    {
    printf("Usage: %s unsfile1 unsfile2 outfile\n", argv[0]);
    exit(0);
    }
n1 = readStudentArray(argv[1],table1,SIZE);
sortStudentArray(table1,n1);
n2 = readStudentArray(argv[2],table2,SIZE);
sortStudentArray(table2,n2);
n3 = mergeStudentArray(table3, table1, n1, table2, n2);
writeStudentArray(argv[3],table3,n3);
}
```

Program 12.7

clean.c — Given as command line parameter a filename, it removes from that file all occurrences of ^M If 'clean' is the executable image of this program, you can use it as follows: % clean dirtyfile > cleanfile

```
#include <stdio.h>
#define CONTROLM 13
int main(int argc, char *argv[])
    {
    char c;
    FILE *fd;
    if(argc!=2)
        {
        printf("Usage: %s filename\n", argv[0]);
        exit(0);
        }
```

```
if((fd = fopen(argv[1],"r"))==NULL)
    {
    perror("fopen");
    exit(1);
    }
while((c=getc(fd))!=EOF)
    if (c!=CONTROLM)
        putchar(c);
fclose(fd);
}
```

Program 12.8

makebinfile.c - Reads a file containing a sequence of text records and writes it out to a new binary files. The names of the files are passed in as command line parameters.

```
#include <stdio.h>
#define SIZE 10
#define NAMESIZE 25
typedef struct {
  char name[NAMESIZE];
  int  midterm;
  int final;
  int homeworks;
} student;
int writeastudent(FILE *fdout, student * who)
   {
  /* Write to an open binary file fdout the content of who.
   * Return the number of bytes that were written out.  */
   char * p;         /* Cursor in outputting a byte at a time */
   char * limit = ((char *)who)+sizeof(student); /*Address just past who */
  for (p=(char *)who;p<limit;p++)
       {
       fputc(*p, fdout);
       }
   return (limit - (char *)who);
```

```
    }
int main (int argc, char *argv[])
    {
    int n = 0;          /* Number of records read */
    int m;              /* Number of bytes in a record */
    student who;        /* Buffer for a record */
    FILE *fdin;         /* File descriptor for input file */
    FILE *fdout;        /* File descriptor for output file */
    if(argc!=3)
        {
        printf("Usage: %s infile outfile\n", argv[0]);
        exit(0);
        }
    if((fdin=fopen(argv[1],"r"))==NULL)
        {
        perror("fopen");
        exit(1);
        }
    if((fdout=fopen(argv[2],"w"))==NULL)
        {
        perror("fopen");
        exit(1);
        }
    while(fscanf(fdin,"%s %d %d %d",
        who.name, &who.midterm, &who.final, &who.homeworks)!=EOF)
        {
        m = writeastudent(fdout, &who);
        printf("m=%d\n", m);
        n++;
        }
    printf("n=%d\n", n);
    fclose(fdin);
    fclose(fdout);
    }
```

PART – IV

Appendix – I
A Complete List of ASCII Symbols

ASCII CHART

Numeric Column – Decimal Number Correspondence Column- Character

0	NUL
1	SOH
2	STX
3	ETX
4	EOT
5	ENQ
6	ACK
7	BEL
8	BS
9	HT
10	LF
11	VT
12	FF
13	CR

14	SO
15	SI
16	DLE
17	DC1
18	DC2
19	DC3
20	DC4
21	NAK
22	SYM
23	ETB
24	CAN
25	EM
26	SUB
27	ESC

28	FS
29	GS
30	RS
31	US
32	SP
33	!
34	“
35	#
36	$
37	%
38	&
39	‘
40	(
41	)

42	*
43	+
44	,
45	-
46	.
47	/
48	0
49	1
50	2
51	3
52	4
53	5
54	6
55	7
56	8
57	9
58	:
59	;
60	<
61	=
62	>
63	?
64	@
65	A
66	B
67	C
68	D
69	E
70	F

71	G
72	H
73	I
74	J
75	K
76	L
77	M
78	N
79	O
80	P
81	Q
82	R
83	S
84	T
85	U
86	V
87	W
88	X
89	Y
90	Z
91	[
92	\
93	]
94	^
95	_
96	`
97	a
98	b
99	c

100	d
101	e
102	f
103	g
104	h
105	i
106	j
107	k
108	l
109	m
110	n
111	o
112	p
113	q
114	r
115	s
116	t
117	u
118	v
119	w
120	x
121	y
122	z
123	{
124	|
125	}
126	~
127	DEL

■■■

Appendix – II
A Complete List of C Keywords and Operators

Operators and Keywords

Operator	Meaning
+	Addition or Unary Plus
–	Subtraction or Unary Minus
*	Multiplication
/	Division
%	Modulus Operator (Remainder)
<	is less than
<=	is less than or equal to
>	is greater than
>=	is greater than or equal to
==	is equal to
!=	is not equal to
&&	Logical AND
||	Logical OR
!	Logical NOT

+=	Plus equal to
-=	Minus equal to
*=	Multiply equal to
/=	Divide equal to
%=	Modulus equal to
++	X++
- -	Y - -
?:	Ternary operator
&	Bitwise AND
|	Bitwise OR
^	Bitwise Exclusive
<<	Shift left
>>	Shift right
Sizeof	Sizeof

Operator Precedence

Order	Category	Operator	Operation	Associativity
1	Highest precedence	( ) [ ] → : : .	Function call	L → R Left to Right
2	Unary	! ~ + - ++ - - & * Size of	Logical negation (NOT) Bitwise 1's complement Unary plus Unary minus Pre or post increment Pre or post decrement Address Indirection Size of operant in bytes	R → L Right -> Left
3	Member Access	.* →*	Dereference Dereference	L → R

Order	Category	Operator	Operation	Associativity
4	Multiplication	*	Multiply	L → R
		/	Divide	
		%	Modulus	
5	Additive	+	Binary Plus	L → R
		-	Binary Minus	
6	Shift	<<	Shift Left	L → R
		>>	Shift Right	
7	Relational	<	Less than	L → R
		<=	Less than or equal to	
		>	Greater than	
		>=	Greater than or equal to	
8	Equality	==	Equal to	L → R
		!=	Not Equal to	
9	Bitwise AAND	&	Bitwise AND	L → R
10	Bitwise XOR	^	Bitwise XOR	L → R
11	Bitwise OR	|	Bitwise OR	L → R
12	Logical AND	&&	Logical AND	L → R
14	Conditional	? :	Ternary Operator	R → L
15	Assignment	=	Assignment	R → L
		*=	Assign product	
		%=	Assign reminder	
		/=	Assign quotient	
		+=	Assign sum	
		-=	Assign difference	
		&=	Assign bitwise AND	
		^=	Assign bitwise XOR	
		|=	Assign bitwise OR	
		<<=	Assign left shift	
		>>=	Assign right shift	

Keywords

Auto	break	Case	char	const	continue	default
Do	double	Else	enum	extern	float	for
Goto	if	Int	long	register	return	short
Signed	sizeof	Static	struct	switch	typedef	union
unsigned	void	Volatile	while			

APPENDIX – III
HEADER-FILEWISE LIST OF ALL FUNCTIONS IN THE C LIBRARY

C Library Functions

Sr. No	Header File	Function	Declaration	Description
1.	assert.h	assert	void assert (int expression);	The assert macro allows diagnostic information to be written to the standard error file.If expression evaluates to 0 (false), then the expression, source code filename, and line number are sent to the standard error, and then calls the abort function.
2.	ctype.h	isalnum();	int isalnum (int character);	a letter (A to Z or a to z) or a digit (0 to 9)
		isalpha();	int isalpha (int character);	a letter (A to Z or a to z)
		iscntrl();	int iscntrl (int character);	any control character (0x00 to 0x1F or 0x7F)

Sr. No	Header File	Function	Declaration	Description
		isdigit();	int isdigit (int character);	a digit (0 to 9)
		isgraph();	int isgraph (int character);	any printing character except for the space character (0x21 to 0x7E)
		islower();	int islower (int character);	a lowercase letter (a to z)
		isprint();	int isprint (int character);	any printing character (0x20 to 0x7E)
		isspace();	int isspace (int character);	a whitespace character (space, tab, carriage return, new line, vertical tab, or formfeed)
		isupper();	int isupper (int character);	an uppercase letter (A to Z)
		isxdigit();	int isxdigit (int character);	a hexadecimal digit (0 to 9, A to F, or a to f)
		tolower();	int tolower (int character);	If the character is an uppercase character (A to Z), then it is converted to lowercase (a to z)
		toupper();	int toupper (int character);	If the character is a lowercase character (a to z), then it is converted to uppercase (A to Z)
3	errno.h	EDOM	#define EDOM some_value	EDOM is an identifier macro declared with #define.
		ERANGE	#define ERANGE some_value	ERANGE is an identifier macro declared with #define.
		Errno	int errno;	
4	float.h		sign value E exponent	The float header defines the minimum and maximum limits of floating-point number values
5	limits.h			The limits header defines the characteristics of variable types.
6	locale.h	Structure	struct lconv	The locale header is useful for setting location specific information.
		Macros	NULL	

Sr. No	Header File	Function	Declaration	Description
			LC_ALL	Set everything
			LC_COLLATE LC_CTYPE	Affects strcoll and strxfrm functions Affects all character functions
			LC_MONETARY	Affects the monetary information provided by localeconv function
			LC_NUMERIC	Affects decimal-point formatting and the information provided by localeconv function
			LC_TIME	Affects the strftime function
		localeconv();	struct lconv *localeconv(void);	Sets the structure lconv to represent the current location settings.
		setlocale();	char *setlocale (int category, const char *locale);	Sets or reads location dependent information.
7	math.h	acos();	double acos (double x);	Returns the arc cosine of x in radians.
		asin();	double asin (double x);	Returns the arc sine of x in radians.
		atan();	double atan (double x);	Returns the arc tangent of x in radians
		atan2();	double atan2 (doubly y, double x);	Returns the arc tangent in radians of y/x based on the signs of both values to determine the correct quadrant.
		ceil();	double ceil (double x);	Returns the smallest integer value greater than or equal to x.
		cos();	double cos (double x);	Returns the cosine of a radian angle x.
		cosh();	double cosh (double x);	Returns the hyperbolic cosine of x.
		exp();	double exp (double x);	Returns the value of e raised to the xth power.
		fabs();	double fabs (double x);	Returns the absolute value of x (a negative value becomes positive, positive value is unchanged).

Sr. No	Header File	Function	Declaration	Description
		floor(); fmod();	double floor (double x); double fmod (double y, double x);	Returns the largest integer value less than or equal to x. Returns the remainder of x divided by y.
		frexp();	double frexp (double x, int *exponent);	The floating-point number x is broken up into a mantissa and exponent.The returned value is the mantissa and the integer pointed to by exponent is the exponent. The resultant value is x=mantissa * 2^exponent.
		ldexp();	double ldexp (double x, int exponent);	Returns x multiplied by 2 raised to the power of exponent.x*2^exponent
		log();	double log (double x);	Returns the natural logarithm (base-e logarithm) of x.
		log10();	double log10 (double x);	Returns the common logarithm (base-10 logarithm) of x.
		modf();	double modf (double x, double *integer);	Breaks the floating-point number x into integer and fraction components.The returned value is the fraction component (part after the decimal), and sets integer to the integer component.
		pow();	double pow (double x, double y);	Returns x raised to the power of y.
		sin();	double sin (double x);	Returns the sine of a radian angle x.
		sinh();	double sinh (double x);	Returns the hyperbolic sine of x.
		sqrt();	double sqrt (double x);	Returns the square root of x.
		tan();	double tan (double x);	Returns the tangent of a radian angle x.
		tanh();	double tanh (double x);	Returns the hyperbolic tangent of x

Sr. No	Header File	Function	Declaration	Description
8	setjmp.h	setjmp();	int setjmp (jmp_buf environment);	Saves the environment into the variable environment. If a non-zero value is returned, then this indicates that the point in the sourcecode was reached by a longjmp. Otherwise zero is returned indicating the environment has been saved.
		longjmp();	void longjmp (jmp_buf environment, int value);	Causes the environment to be restored from a setjmp call where the environment variable had been saved
9	signal.h	Macros:		Default handler.
		SIG_DFL		
		SIG_ERR		Represents a signal error.
		SIG_IGN		Signal ignore.
		SIGABRT		Abnormal termination (generated by the abort function).
		SIGFPE		Floating-point error (error caused by division by zero, invalid operation, etc.).
		SIGILL		Illegal operation (instruction).
		SIGINT		Interactive attention signal (such as ctrl-C).
		SIGSEGV		Invalid access to storage (segment violation, memory violation).
		SIGTERM		Termination request.
		signal();	void (*signal(int sig, void (*func) (int)))(int);	Controls how a signal is handled. sig represents the signal number compatible with the SIG macros. func is the function to be called when the signal occurs.
		raise();	int raise(int sig);	Causes signal sig to be generated. The sig argument is compatible with the SIG macros.

Sr. No	Header File	Function	Declaration	Description
10	stdarg.h	va_start();	void va_start (va_list ap, last_arg);	Initializes ap for use with the va_arg and va_end macros. last_arg is the last known fixed argument being passed to the function
		va_arg();	type va_arg (va_list ap, type);	Expands to the next argument in the paramater list of the function with type type.
		va_end();	void va_end (va_list ap);	Allows a function with variable arguments which used the va_start macro to return.
11	stddef.h	offsetof();	offsetof(type, member-designator)	This results in a constant integer of type size_t which is the offset in bytes of a structure member from the beginning of the structure.
12	stdio.h	_IOFBF _IOLBF _IONBF	_IOFBF, _IOLBF, and _IONBF are used in the setvbuf function.	
		BUFSIZ	BUFSIZ is an integer which represents the size of the buffer used by the setbuf function.	
		EOF	EOF is a negative integer which indicates an end-of-file has been reached.	
		FOPEN_ MAX	FOPEN_MAX is an integer which represents the maximum number of files that the system can guarantee that can be opened simultaneously.	
		FILENAME_ MAX	FILENAME_MAX is an integer which represents the longest length of a char array suitable for holding the longest possible filename.	
		L_tmpnam	L_tmpnam is an integer which represents the longest length of a char array suitable for holding the longest possible temporary filename created by the tmpnam function.	
		SEEK_CUR SEEK_END SEEK_SET	SEEK_CUR, SEEK_END, and SEEK_SET are used in the fseek function.	
		TMP_MAX	TMP_MAX is the maximum number of unique filenames that the function tmpnam can generate.	

Sr. No	Header File	Function	Declaration	Description
		stderr stdin stdout	stderr, stdin, and stdout are pointers to FILE types which correspond to the standard error, standard input, and standard output streams.	
		clearerr();	void clearerr (FILE *stream);	Clears the end-of-file and error indicators for the given stream.
		fclose();	int fclose (FILE *stream);	Closes the stream. All buffers are flushed.
		feof();	int feof (FILE *stream);	Tests the end-of-file indicator for the given stream.
		ferror();	int ferror (FILE *stream);	Tests the error indicator for the given stream.
		fflush();	int fflush (FILE *stream);	Flushes the output buffer of a stream.
		fgetpos();	int fgetpos (FILE *stream, fpos_t *pos);	Gets the current file position of the stream and writes it to pos.
		fopen();	FILE *fopen (const char *filename, const char *mode);	Opens the filename pointed to by filename.
		fread();	size_t fread(void *ptr, size_t size, size_t nmemb, FILE *stream);	Reads data from the given stream into the array pointed to by ptr.
		freopen();	FILE *freopen (const char *filename, const char *mode, FILE *stream);	Associates a new filename with the given open stream.
		fseek();	int fseek (FILE *stream, long int offset, int whence);	Sets the file position of the stream to the given offset.

Sr. No	Header File	Function	Declaration	Description
		fsetpos();	int fsetpos (FILE *stream, const fpos_t *pos);	Sets the file position of the given stream to the given position.
		ftell();	long int ftell (FILE *stream);	Returns the current file position of the given stream.
		fwrite();	size_t fwrite (const void *ptr, size_t size, size_t nmemb, FILE *stream);	Writes data from the array pointed to by ptr to the given stream.
		remove();	int remove(const char *filename);	Deletes the given filename so that it is no longer accessible
		rename();	int rename (const char *old_filename, const char *new_filename);	Causes the filename referred to by old_filename to be changed to new_filename.
		rewind();	void rewind (FILE *stream);	Sets the file position to the beginning of the file of the given stream.
		setbuf();	void setbuf (FILE *stream, char *buffer);	Defines how a stream should be buffered.
		setvbuf();	int setvbuf (FILE *stream, char *buffer, int mode, size_t size);	Defines how a stream should be buffered
		tmpfile();	FILE *tmpfile(void);	Creates a temporary file in binary update mode (wb+). The tempfile is removed when the program terminates or the stream is closed.
		tmpnam();	char *tmpnam (char *str);	Generates and returns a valid temporary filename which does not exist.

Sr. No	Header File	Function	Declaration	Description
		fprintf();	int fprintf(FILE *stream, const char *format, ...);	sends formatted output to a stream
		fscanf();	int fscanf(FILE *stream, const char *format,...);	reads formatted input from a stream
		printf();	int printf(const char *format, ...);	sends formatted output to stdout
		scanf();	int scanf(const char *format, ...);	reads formatted input from stdin
		sprintf();	int sprintf(char *str, const char *format, ...);	sends formatted output to a string
		sscanf();	int sscanf(const char *str, const char *format,...);	reads formatted input from a string
		vfprintf();	int vfprintf(FILE *stream, const char *format, va_list arg);	sends formatted output to a stream using an argument list
		vprintf();	int vprintf(const char *format, va_list arg);;	sends formatted output to stdout using an argument list
		vsprintf();	int vsprintf(char *str, const char *format, va_list arg)	sends formatted output to a string using an argument list
		fgetc();	int fgetc(FILE *stream);	Gets the next character (an unsigned char) from the specified stream and advances the position indicator for the stream.
		fgets();	char *fgets(char *str, int n, FILE *stream);	Reads a line from the specified stream and stores it into the string pointed to by str.

Sr. No	Header File	Function	Declaration	Description
		fputc();	int fputc(int char, FILE *stream);	Writes a character (an unsigned char) specified by the argument char to the specified stream and advances the position indicator for the stream.
		fputs();	int fputs(const char *str, FILE *stream);	Writes a string to the specified stream up to but not including the null character.
		getc();	int getc(FILE *stream);	Gets the next character (an unsigned char) from the specified stream and advances the position indicator for the stream.
		getchar();	int getchar(void);	Gets a character (an unsigned char) from stdin.
		gets();	char *gets (char *str);	Reads a line from stdin and stores it into the string pointed to by str.
		putc();	int putc(int char, FILE *stream);	Writes a character (an unsigned char) specified by the argument char to the specified stream and advances the position indicator for the stream.
		putchar();	int putchar (int char);	Writes a character (an unsigned char) specified by the argument char to stdout.
		puts();	int puts (const char *str);	Writes a string to stdout up to but not including the null character.
		ungetc();	int ungetc(int char, FILE *stream);	Pushes the character char (an unsigned char) onto the specified stream so that the this is the next character read.
		perror();	void perror(const char *str);	Prints a descriptive error message to stderr.
13	stdlib.h	abort();	void abort(void);	Causes an abnormal program termination.
		abs();	int abs(int x);	Returns the absolute value of x.

Sr. No	Header File	Function	Declaration	Description
		atexit();	int atexit(void (*func)(void));	Causes the specified function to be called when the program terminates normally.
		atof();	double atof(const char *str);	The string pointed to by the argument str is converted to a floating-point number (type double).
		atoi();	int atoi(const char *str);	The string pointed to by the argument str is converted to an integer (type int).
		atol();	long int atol(const char *str);	The string pointed to by the argument str is converted to a long integer
		bsearch();	void *bsearch (const void *key, const void *base, size_t nitems, size_t size, int (*compar) (const void *, const void *));	Performs a binary search.
		calloc();	void *calloc (size_t nitems, size_t size);	Allocates the requested memory and returns a pointer to it.
		div();	div_t div(int numer, int denom);	Divides numer (numerator) by denom (denominator).
		free();	void free (void *ptr);	Deallocates the memory previously allocated by a call to calloc, malloc, or realloc.
		exit();	void exit (int status);	Causes the program to terminate normally.
		getenv();	char *getenv (const char *name);	Searches for the environment string pointed to by name and returns the associated value to the string.
		labs();	long int labs(long int x);	Returns the absolute value of x.

Sr. No	Header File	Function	Declaration	Description
		ldiv();	ldiv_t ldiv(long int numer, long int denom);	Divides numer (numerator) by denom (denominator).
		malloc();	void *malloc (size_t size);	Allocates the requested memory and returns a pointer to it.
		mblen();	int mblen(const char *str, size_t n);	Returns the length of a multibyte character pointed to by the argument str.
		mbstowcs();	size_t mbstowcs (schar_t *pwcs, const char *str, size_t n);	Converts the string of multibyte characters pointed to by the argument str to the array pointed to by pwcs.
		mbtowc();	int mbtowc (whcar_t *pwc, const char *str, size_t n);	Examines the multibyte character pointed to by the argument str.
		qsort();	void qsort(void *base, size_t nitems, size_t size, int (*compar) (const void *, const void*));	Sorts an array.
		rand();	int rand(void);	Returns a pseudo-random number in the range of 0 to RAND_MAX.
		realloc();	void *realloc(void *ptr, size_t size);	Attempts to resize the memory block pointed to by ptr that was previously allocated with a call to malloc or calloc.
		srand();	void srand (unsigned int seed);	This function seeds the random number generator used by the function rand.
		strtod();	double strtod (const char *str, char **endptr);	The string pointed to by the argument str is converted to a floating-point number

Sr. No	Header File	Function	Declaration	Description
		strtol();	long int strtol (const char *str, char **endptr, int base);	The string pointed to by the argument str is converted to a long integer (type long int).
		strtoul();	unsigned long int strtoul(const char *str, char **endptr, int base);	The string pointed to by the argument str is converted to an unsigned long integer (type unsigned long int).
		system();	int system(const char *string);	The command specified by string is passed to the host environment to be executed by the command processor.
		wcstombs();	size_t wcstombs (char *str, const wchar_t *pwcs, size_t n);	Converts the codes stored in the array pwcs to multibyte characters and stores them in the string str.
		wctomb();	int wctomb(char *str, wchar_t wchar);	Examines the code which corresponds to a multibyte character given by the argument wchar.
13.	string.h	memchr();	void *memchr (const void *str, int c, size_t n);	Searches for the first occurrence of the character c (an unsigned char) in the first n bytes of the string pointed to by the argument str.
		memcmp();	int memcmp (const void *str1, const void *str2, size_t n);	Compares the first n bytes of str1 and str2. Does not stop comparing even after the null character (it always checks n characters).
		memcpy();	void *memcpy (void *str1, const void *str2, size_t n);	Copies n characters from str2 to str1. If str1 and str2 overlap the behavior is undefined.

Sr. No	Header File	Function	Declaration	Description
		memmove();	void *memmove (void *str1, const void *str2, size_t n);	Copies n characters from str2 to str1.
		memset();	void *memset (void *str, int c, size_t n);	Copies the character c (an unsigned char) to the first n characters of the string pointed to by the argument str.
		strcat();	char *strcat(char *str1, const char *str2);	Appends the string pointed to by str2 to the end of the string pointed to by str1.
		strncat();	char *strncat(char *str1, const char *str2, size_t n);	Appends the string pointed to by str2 to the end of the string pointed to by str1 up to n characters long.
		strchr();	char *strchr(const char *str, int c);	Searches for the first occurrence of the character c (an unsigned char) in the string pointed to by the argument str.
		strcmp();	int strcmp(const char *str1, const char *str2);	Compares the string pointed to by str1 to the string pointed to by str2.
		strncmp();	int strncmp(const char *str1, const char *str2, size_t n);	Compares at most the first n bytes of str1 and str2. Stops comparing after the null character.
		strcoll();	int strcoll(const char *str1, const char *str2);	Compares string str1 to str2. The result is dependent on the LC_COLLATE setting of the location.
		strcpy();	char *strcpy(char *str1, const char *str2);	Copies the string pointed to by str2 to str1.
		strncpy();	char *strncpy (char *str1, const char *str2, size_t n);	Copies up to n characters from the string pointed to by str2 to str1.

Sr. No	Header File	Function	Declaration	Description
		strcspn();	size_t strcspn (const char *str1, const char *str2);	Finds the first sequence of characters in the string str1 that does not contain any character specified in str2.
		strlen();	size_t strlen (const char *str);	Computes the length of the string str up to but not including the terminating null character.
		strpbrk();	char *strpbrk (const char *str1, const char *str2);	Finds the first character in the string str1 that matches any character specified in str2.
		strrchr();	char *strrchr (const char *str, int c);	Searches for the last occurrence of the character c (an unsigned char) in the string pointed to by the argument str. The terminating null character is considered to be part of the string.
		strspn();	size_t strspn (const char *str1, const char *str2);	Finds the first sequence of characters in the string str1 that contains any character specified in str2.
		strstr();	char *strstr (const char *str1, const char *str2);	Finds the first occurrence of the entire string str2 (not including the terminating null character) which appears in the string str1.
		strtok();	char *strtok (char *str1, const char *str2);	Breaks string str1 into a series of tokens. If str1 and str2 are not null, then the following search sequence begins.
		strxfrm();	size_t strxfrm (char *str1, const char *str2, size_t n);	Transforms the string str2 and places the result into str1.
		strerror();	char *strerror (int errnum);	Searches an internal array for the error number errnum and returns a pointer to an error message string.

Sr. No	Header File	Function	Declaration	Description
14	time.h	asctime();	char *asctime (const struct tm *timeptr);	Returns a pointer to a string which represents the day and time of the structure timeptr.
		clock();	clock_t clock(void);	Returns the processor clock time used since the beginning of an implementation-defined era (normally the beginning of the program).
		ctime();	char *ctime (const time_t *timer);	Returns a string representing the localtime based on the argument timer.
		difftime();	double difftime (time_t time1, time_t time2);	Calculates the difference of seconds between time1 and time2 (time1-time2). Returns the number of seconds.
		gmtime();	struct tm *gmtime (const time_t *timer);	The value of timer is broken up into the structure tm and expressed in Coordinated Universal Time (UTC) also known as Greenwich Mean Time (GMT).
		localtime();	struct tm *localtime(const time_t *timer);	The value of timer is broken up into the structure tm and expressed in the local time zone.
		mktime();	time_t mktime (struct tm *timeptr);	Converts the structure pointed to by timeptr into a time_t value according to the local time zone.
		strftime();	size_t strftime (char *str, size_t maxsize, const char *format, const struct tm *timeptr);	Formats the time represented in the structure timeptr according to the formatting rules defined in format and stored into str. No more than maxsize characters are stored into str (including the terminating null character).
		time();	time_t time (time_t *timer);	Calculates the current calender time and encodes it into time_t format.

■ ■ ■